How to Upgrade & Motivate Your Cleaning Crews

By Don Aslett

Don Aslett flying somewhere!

Don's Books

Don Aslett's home in the hills.

VARSITY CONTRACTORS WORLD HEADQUARTERS

Marsh Creek PRESS

DON ASLETT'S CLEANING CENTER

DON ASLETT'S CLEANING MUSEUM & Library

How to Upgrade & Motivate Your Cleaning Crews

Published by Marsh Creek Press, PO Box 700, Pocatello, Idaho 83204 1-208-232-3535.

ISBN 0-937750-06-9

Illustrator: Kerry Otteson
Editor: Carol Cartaino
Production Manager: Tobi Flynn

The ideas and descriptions in this book are meant to share my company's most successful motivational techniques and events with you, and to inspire you to create your own. Neither I nor Varsity Contractors, however, can be responsibile for any mishaps that might occur at any janitor event or gathering modeled after anything in these pages. Always remember safety first, and plan and prepare all your activities accordingly.

JANUS ® is a registered trademark of the PortionPac Chemical Corporation.

MARSH CREEK PRESS

To Marvin Klein

This book is dedicated to one of the leaders in our industry, Marvin Klein. Marvin, through example, innovation, and inspiration, has consistently promoted a deserved high status for custodians.

"It will take time, but with each of us actively promoting a positive image of our industry, we can change the attitude of the public and management.

The result will be a proud, successful, and professional housekeeping/maintenance industry. Remember, it is *our* image and *our* future that is on the line!"

—Marvin Klein

How To Upgrade & Motivate Your Cleaning Crews

Table of Contents

Preface

Chapter 1
A Cleaner (janitor, custodian, maid, etc.): Why Would Anyone Want to Be One? ..5

Chapter 2
Uplift: A Profession That Needs a Lot of It! 7

Chapter 3
Say it Loud: I'm a Janitor and I'm Proud! 12

Chapter 4
How You Can Provide That All-Important Identity 16

Chapter 5
Complaints: The Pro Cleaner's #1 Confidence Killer 35

Chapter 6
Motivation in the Heart of the Job 42

Chapter 7
Motivating in the Meat and Potato Issues 51

Chapter 8
Janitorize Your Life! (or: Living the Religion of "Clean") 58

Chapter 9
Awards Make Motivation Easy, Don't They? 69

Chapter 10
Janitor Special Events 77

Chapter 11
Varsity Candid Shots 114

Upgrade & Motivate Your Cleaning Crews

I kept this book short and simple because I know that with just a glimpse at these ideas you will know what to do to bring the feelings of love and motivation, and a brighter image into the cleaning ranks.

Your reward...

Will be that people—even people who are making good money at other jobs—start requesting to come to work in your department. Then you'll know you are getting the image-lifting job done.

I'm proud to be associated with all of you who call yourselves cleaners. You have my commitment that I am going to work and study and strive to get better and better and lift the cleaning profession higher and higher, find ever more ways to build and perpetuate the image of "clean."

Sincerely,
King of the Toilet Ring
Fastest Bowl Brush in the West
Billy Graham of the Pine-Sol Set
The Porcelain Preacher
The Pied Piper of Purification
Johnny-on-the-Spot
Baron of the Biffy
Captain Commode
Dean of Clean
Janitor of the Jet Set
Commodian
The Phyllis Diller of Toilets
Monsieur of Messes
Professor of the Potty
Titan of the Toilet Bowl
Flush Gordon
Minstrel of the Mop
Guru of the Loo

—Don Aslett

Preface

It's easy to teach people cleaning techniques, but it's hard to teach and convince them to have a good attitude about it. After all, the janitor image is of a nobody, the hours are tough, the pay is low, and the rewards—well, the rewards almost seem to be nonexistent.

No wonder we often fail to motivate and so pay the price with poor productivity and high turnover. The cleaning industry today has an average 300% turnover annually; 96% of new cleaning businesses fail; and too many cleaning or maintenance people only work at this job until **something better comes along.**

We have to manage to upgrade and motivate our employees in a profession that constantly has to redo its work. Work that never seems to be appreciated. And in a situation where people always take the positive for granted and report only the negative. That's why we need motivation so badly!

Running a successful cleaning business for more than 40 years now, and employing thousands of people to clean for a living, has given me a lot of insight into the minds and hearts of janitors. How they work, how they feel, how they do their jobs, what makes them get up in the morning, what excites them, how they see the world and themselves. It's clear to me why professionals suffer the low self-image that seems to characterize our industry. I'm convinced we can affect the way the public (and upper management) see janitors by changing the way they see themselves.

And by making others aware that

"CLEANERS"
(janitors, maids, custodians, etc.)
are true professionals and human beings, not robots or commodities.

As "America's Number One Cleaning Expert" and someone who built a 100+ million dollar cleaning company from scratch on the strength of the enthusiasm and excellence of its employees, I've written this book to help you implement a motivation campaign for your janitors.

Most motivation attempts are like pouring a little gasoline into the carburetor when your car is out of gas. You get a few chugs and then it almost turns over, but before you know it, it dies out. Most motivation is temporary, it doesn't have the momentum to continue on its own. Magic formulas aren't the answer, neither is bribing a janitor with a gold key or a grandiose certificate.

Motivation has to come from within, it can't just be external expressions—awards or trinkets, or a new piece of equipment every few years. Morale building and motivation comes from actions, not talk and thank-you speeches.

I have firsthand, frontline experience of what really works, and what

doesn't when it comes to encouraging your custodians. In 1985 I gathered this information together into a little booklet called "How to Upgrade & Motivate Your Cleaning Crews." It contained the approach and secrets that have made my own company, Varsity Contractors, Inc., one of the most unique and energetic forces in the cleaning industry. After I published it, two things happened:

1. People loved the book and bought thousands of copies,
2. Many of those who read the book sent me their ideas.

And so I put together this new edition of How to Upgrade & Motivate. I think you'll find it to be the most effective tool you've ever had for preventing wasted time and money. It will also stimulate and encourage your own ideas to flow. The upshot is you'll end up with a cleaner building and a happier crew.

Motivated people make all the difference.

A Cleaner

(janitor, custodian, maid, etc.): Why Would Anyone Want to Be One?

Every single person in the world has asked himself that question. (Most of us mutter it to ourselves while doing our housework.)

After all, cleaning has some pretty negative connotations:

• Parents punish their kids with it: "If you don't clean your plate, you'll have to clean your room!"

• Teachers threaten pupils with it: "You better study hard or you'll end up like Mr. Smith—a custodian!"

• Even bosses use it against employees: "Hey Mac, if you can't cut it here, there's always room in Janitorial!"

Time after time we janitors are relegated to the bottom of the barrel. The cleaning profession is about the least impressive career going.

A cleaner enters a field with low self-esteem, and then he's only further discouraged by what he faces from the public. We all seem to forget what it feels like to be a janitor—even a seasoned veteran of the janitorial business like me has to be reminded.

One janitor's daily report sums it up well:

The kids peed on the piano keys last night. It was a real struggle getting it off. Two nights ago they did it on the heat radiator, that's where the stink came from that everyone was complaining about. I found a dead salmon in one of the lockers today. Six wastebaskets had a half-cup of coffee in each of them again—I caught the first five—the last one spilled. I spent two hours of my own time removing spots. Three toilets were plugged up on purpose—I had to go in with the old hands this time. (These were the type of stop-ups that could easily have been avoided in an all-adult building). Then there was the mess from someone getting hand dryers hot and shooting hair spray in them, turning them into blowtorches. Supplies were missing out of my closet, so I had to bring a vacuum from home again to clean. Found a note telling me to shampoo the conference room carpet tonight, "Sorry for the late notice." Another message— two of the crew are sick, I'll have to do their work.

This excerpt from my old files should convince us of the reality of the need to understand, build up and

motivate our cleaning people. Motivating employees is a managerial skill that almost always needs improving. Unmotivated cleaners do slow and mediocre work and never achieve professionalism. An unmotivated cleaner can stretch a 2-hour task into an 8-hour shift—and then groan and moan and bellyache if you ask him/her to do 15 minutes of anything additional.

The so often overlooked act of motivating and improving your people's self-image can mean a 30% decrease in supply costs and a 40% improvement in work quality. Plus a lot fewer complaints.

Look at what happy, motivated, and satisfied cleaning people do for you:

• **They're loyal:** That means they don't cheat, they don't abuse absenteeism, they won't steal from you, and they represent you well to your customers.

• **They stay:** That means your turnover drops—which means you'll be able to spend less time replacing people, and cut down on expensive training sessions, and sometimes even unemployment taxes.

• **They produce:** Motivated employees clean twice as much and twice as well as other cleaners. When your people have the desire to work fast and efficiently they will, because their work is exciting… and they know they're an important cog in the machinery of the facility.

• **They cut building depreciation:** It's not unusual for a carpet to last 10 or 15 years, but in a building cleaned by uncaring custodians, it may last only 3 years. The savings in structure and furnishings depreciation with motivated cleaners can amount to thousands of dollars a year. For the most part, motivating your crews costs you little or nothing, and gives you a much greater return on your investment in your company and your employees. This book will give you a lot of ways to begin. And believe me, once you get started it will spark a hundred other ideas of your own.

2 Uplift: A Profession That Needs a Lot of It!

WET FLOOR

People get speeding tickets going to ball games, concerts, weddings, fishing, even on their way to work. But have you ever heard of a janitor speeding to work and getting a traffic ticket? Hmmmmm…

Professional cleaners come up against some pretty discouraging conditions. It's not the work itself—scrubbing, sweeping, and mopping even the dirtiest, dingiest area—that's not the problem. It's the attitude and circumstance that surrounds it. Let's take a look at some of the janitor's biggest hang-ups, before we consider the cures.

Whether the work we do is physical or mental, it's in our very nature to build something indelible. Mankind always works and strives to build something enduring—a reputation, a career, a family, a structure, a relationship—everything we do, we want to make it last. Look at the pyramids: all that labor and sacrifice left a monument that has lasted for more than 4500 years and awed generation after generation. Through the ages man has built things to last and to have an impact. We want to make our mark on this earth, that's what it's all about, and what makes all our efforts worthwhile.

Cleaning goes against the very grain of this instinct. Cleaning, at best, lasts for maybe 24 hours. The minute it's done, it's undone. We can clean and sweep and service and leave a blinding shine on the floors, but within hours you can't even tell we were there. Cleaning is like changing diapers, sometimes it only lasts a second, until all that work is pooped away.

While other workers set goals and look forward to starting and progressing on new projects, and achieving some kind of recognition when those projects are complete, a janitor knows that with the next flush, all his efforts are down the drain. So we go back and do it again, and again.

Sure, it's our job to renew the place and sure, we're thankful for the work, but the point is, what if after you built a dam or a building or a pyramid, within 24 hours someone demolished it and you had to start over? What if day after day your work was destroyed? All eight hours of it, gone. What if you had to start every morning not an inch ahead of where you were yesterday and not an inch ahead of where you'll be tomorrow? How many days would you smilingly and cheerfully come to work? Well, that's a janitor's lot.

In most jobs, there's a light at the end of the tunnel, a peak, a victory, a **finish**, but in the cleaning field it's difficult to see. Even if you're promoted to head cleaner, the toilets aren't any less filthy or the floors less littered.

To the office worker arriving for work in the morning it's obvious that some time during the night the cleaning people have been there doing their jobs. That's the status quo— clean is expected, in fact super-clean is expected, but the only time the cleaners get any feedback from the tenants is when something is missed, or hasn't been cleaned or emptied. The public takes all the positive for granted and reports only the negative.

Three thousand times the faithful phantoms of the night will empty and clean and replace the wastebasket just right, and nothing is said. Thanks are seldom heard and rarely written. But on the three thousand and first time, the wastebasket is accidentally left on the desk or the wrong side of the room, or the soap dispenser is empty, and the tenant comes unglued. If anything is broken or missing, the janitor is the prime—often the only— suspect and must answer for it, whether or not he or she was even on that particular shift.

As a professional consultant, I'm often asked to fly to a school, factory, or other establishment, where management asks me to "shape up and motivate" the janitors! Surprisingly, I often find that the manager, owner, superintendent, supervisor—the leaders—are the most serious problem. Take five honest minutes and fill in this self-evaluation of your motivating merit and see how you fare:

20 Questions to Measure the Morale & Motivation of Your Cleaning Crews

	NEVER	SELDOM	AVERAGE	ALWAYS
1. Cleaners are known and called by their first names	0	1	3	5
2. They study and improve themselves	0	1	3	5
3. They volunteer for extra jobs	0	1	3	5
4. They have and wear uniforms	0	1	3	5
5. They have and wear name tags	0	1	3	5
6. Crews are well groomed and dressed	0	1	3	5
7. They are on time and don't leave early	0	1	3	5
8. They receive training, encouragement, and inspiration	0	1	3	5
9. Their closets and equipment are clean and well kept	0	1	3	5
10. Products are up to date and crews understand how to use them	0	1	3	5
11. Exact cleaning times, places, frequencies are recorded by crew	0	1	3	5
12. They have an effective inspection/quality control program	0	1	3	5
13. They have a bonus or incentive program	0	1	3	5
14. They receive praise and compliments from tenants and customers	0	1	3	5
15. They bring pictures, decorations to the bulletin board	0	1	3	5
16. They are involved in company, client, or school social events	0	1	3	5
17. They understand their job future	0	1	3	5
18. They attend seminars and inservice workshops	0	1	3	5
19. They encourage (tenants/students) to help keep the building clean	0	1	3	5
20. Custodians/Supervisors have personal business cards	0	1	3	5

Circle your answer, then add up all the numbers for your score.

0-25 Don't be surprised to come in one morning and find your employees have mutinied!

51-75 Not bad… but not great. The potential is there for a sharp work crew if you keep up the training.

26-50 They're only sticking around because "It's a paycheck…" and their work shows it.

76-100 They're knowledgeable, dedicated, diligent, and disciplined… you and your crew should be proud!

3 Say it Loud:

I'm a Janitor and I'm Proud!

You're sitting down at Sunday dinner, and one of your guests is admiring your bright, good-looking son.

"How old are you? What's your favorite subject in school?" The questions go on and on, until they reach the big one: "What are you going to be when you grow up?"

Your son's eyes widen, his face brightens, and he blurts out, "A janitor!"

"A janitor!" They gasp, caught totally off guard. They're taken aback and scarcely know what to say or how to react.

"Why would you ever want to be a janitor?"

"Because they take care of large and important public places, enhance the quality of life, help maintain health and safety, save energy, retard depreciation, and create good public relations for the business community."

GOOD ANSWER, KID!

So your son grows up. He's a star athlete in the local high school, then he fulfills his goal and becomes a janitor. Now when friends ask, "What's your redheaded Olympic hopeful up to these days?"

You stutter and sputter and say, "Ah, um… he works in the big buildings downtown."

"Great, what's he do?"

"Ahhh, he makes them healthy," you cough and mumble, "he's a pollution control engineer."

POOR ANSWER, FOLKS!

The name—the label: janitor, is a

legitimate one. You won't change the position just by changing the name—you can't change the contents of a package by changing the label. All the new equipment or technical advancement in the world isn't likely to change the basic nature of the janitor's job. Trying to upgrade the image of cleaning by making up fancy titles is a mistake.

"Janitor" clearly identifies the job and cuts through all the confusion.

Janitor is by no means a title without class or tradition. It comes from the God Janus, one of the most important deities worshipped by the ancient Romans. Janus was the god of entrances and exits, of sunrise and sunset. He's usually depicted as having two faces—one looking forward and one back (see p. 60). Prayers were made to Janus at the beginning of any important undertaking.

In every home, the first morning prayers were addressed to him. His aid was sought not only for national problems like war or political crisis, but also for personal and household undertakings. As the god of beginnings he was, logically enough, also the God of the New Year, as well as the first month of the new year. From him, we

get the word "January." He was also the god who ruled over progress and civilization. From all of this you can see why he was the official caretaker and custodian of Roman homes and estates … their special deity, you might say. And it's from the god Janus that the word "janitor" originated.

Yet personnel departments and industrial psychologists are constantly trying to restyle the straightforward term janitor into a "more socially acceptable" title.

What Do These Titles Really Mean?

Matron:
women's prison guard? dowager?
Porter:
luggage handler? furniture mover?
Custodian:
someone who watches over wards of the court?
Attendant:
parking lot attendant? valet?
Houservice person:
butler? jack of all trades?
Housekeeping:
laundry? cooking? in a hospital?
Sanitation Engineer:
toilet designer? sewer builder?
Cleaner:
dry cleaner? drape service?
Maid?
lady in waiting
Dustman? Char?

There's no end to the confusion and trouble that comes from dodging the direct approach, or pretending to be something you're not. During an interview on British television once the host asked me, "Just what do you do in America, Mr. Aslett?"

Sidestepping the word "janitor," I said, "Oh, I'm just an old scrubber from Idaho."

Gasps from the audience made me realize I'd said something wrong. Later they told me that in England a scrubber is a hooker—a prostitute! Imagine what 5 million viewers thought.

Changing the label doesn't fool anyone. We say queen size or portly for plain old big and fat. We call the city dump a sanitary landfill, but it doesn't change how it smells. Glorifying the title is an illusion that's easy to see through, like a window washer calling himself a transparent surface maintenance engineer.

Trying to "title" the nature of the job away is about as silly as the story a telephone company psychologist told me about a husband and wife who cleaned the phone company's Manhattan skyscraper. They lived about 35 miles upstate in a nice upper-class neighborhood. Every morning they'd dress up elegantly and drive their Cadillac to the commuter train. Then when they arrived at work, they changed into their uniforms to do their jobs: he cleaned the bathrooms and she cleaned the cafeteria.

With tenure and skill they each made around $30,000, which meant $60,000 between them, a good family income in that day. They told the personnel manager emphatically that if he ever told any caller, credit checker, or anyone (kids not excluded) exactly what their jobs were, they would sue the company. The upstate neighborhood knew only that the Hansons worked for the phone com-

pany in the prestigious downtown building. The Hansons of course were only kidding themselves. For sure, 99% of the time, everyone is going to know sooner or later what you actually do—clean or compute, try cases or cut meat. It's inevitable.

A janitor is a janitor is a janitor—they always will be. They clean up after people. If you think a grand and glorious title will motivate your cleaning crew, you're only fooling yourself, because you sure won't fool them. Some positions have such flowery titles, even the boss isn't sure what the job is.

Instead, use the title we already have with pride. It's the first step in upgrading the image of your cleaning people—call them what they are. Use the label prominently and naturally in your business, put it right up there with doctor, lawyer, and chef. It's a legitimate occupation—and for that matter, a profession. Like any profession it takes training and skill.

Janitors are People, Not Mop-Wielding Robots!

Have you ever noticed that the public has a tendency to treat janitors, waitresses, and most service people like fixtures, like they're not even there? People will talk about intimate things in the presence of the cleaning people. They'll say embarrassing things or leave out personal items as if the service crew can't hear or understand, making it clear that those who wait on others are either retarded, deaf or dumb, or just don't matter much anyway....

Not long ago, for example, while one of our top janitors (a well-educated, attractive grandmother) was cleaning the men's restroom, a brusque businessman came in and used the urinal right next to the one that she was cleaning. Neither said a word, but he clearly implied "You are a nothing—you don't see, feel, or have any sense of decency I need to be concerned with." He didn't even acknowledge that she existed as another human being... because she was a cleaner.

How would that make you feel about your job?

We ourselves are often guilty of treating our own people in the very same impersonal way. We deal with them as a division or crew instead of as individuals. We send messages and leave notes instead of making a personal contact. We discourage friendliness. When absenteeism occurs we reflexively express concern for the work missed before showing concern for the employee's welfare.

Do you or any of your staff really know the janitor? Sure you can point out someone and say, "That's the janitor," and that's the point. How often do you point out the engineer, the accountant, or others without first identifying them by their names? The janitor seems to have no personal identity and identity is what we each crave above all. There's a person in there, a real live human being, with feelings, problems, needs, and ambitions; a person who wants to be noticed, praised, and appreciated like the rest of us. Give your cleaners a little personal attention and watch them come alive. Talk to them and with them—you'll discover that many of them have a wide variety of experiences to share. I know of one school janitor who has his master's degree and over twelve years of experience in the classroom as a teacher of English. Dull, uneducated, incompetent? NO— he just wanted a change and a little solitude.

Try greeting your janitor by name rather than a nod and make even those brief snatches of conversation count: "How's the baby?" "How's Bill doing in college?" "The building never looked better...."

4 How You Can Provide That All-Important Identity

WET FLOOR

The mystery of "the elves that come in to clean in the night" is one of the ways janitors lose their identity.

Switch some of the crew to daytime service once in a while if you can, so they can see things in the light and the customers, and other departments can see the people who've been doing all the cleaning. The upgrading result will be unmistakable.

If no one is ever around to see the cleaners perform their duties, maybe they really don't exist—they truly are phantoms in the night! Schedule some cleaning during business hours. We did that in a million-square-foot complex and watched public relations go up and complaints go down.

Even if you can't arrange some prime-time cleaning, you can bring the janitor in as often as possible to interact with the other employees. Invite your janitors to participate in company activities and company-sponsored civic causes: blood donation drives, United Way Campaign, etc.

When someone new is added to the staff or to the building, in any department, take the cleaners to them or them to the cleaning crew for introductions. This is **never** done, even though every last office worker down to the part-time typist is given a big introduction. The cleaners are generally considered fixtures, and pretty soon they even start to act like fixtures.

Business Cards

Ever thought about printing cards for your cleaning people? They cost next to nothing, and you may find a savings in having the company logo pre-printed in bulk. Cards are handy and effective for leaving messages and soliciting business, and even more important, a business card is an identity.

The front of my own business card reads:

Hi... I'm Don Aslett! I'm from Pocatello, Idaho. You're probably wondering about my strange luggage. It's not a porta-potty, it's my suitcase. Why do I carry a toilet suitcase? Well, doctors carry their little black bags; lawyers and business executives carry their attache cases; and I, a professional cleaner, carry a toilet suitcase. The toilet which I (along with 8,000,000 janitors and 50,000,000 homemakers) clean regularly, is a symbol of my trade. I carry it to dispel any doubt as to how I feel about my profession—I'm proud of it.

I've been nicknamed by the media: *The Porcelain Preacher, The Billy Graham of the Pine-Sol Set, King of the Toilet Ring, The Urinal Colonel, Pied Piper of Purification, Baron of the Biffy, Fastest Bowl Brush in the West* ... and others.

Some say I'm a janitor because a twelfth-century relative of mine was Duke of the Royal Chamber Pot. Not so, it wasn't blood lines that got me into the cleaning business, it was red-blooded American enterprise!

Uniforms

What if, at the next professional football game, none of the players or referees wore uniforms and instead came out wearing a wild variety of sweatsuits, t-shirts, cutoffs, Levis, etc. The fans might get the same quality game, the same players and plays, the same thrills and excitement of pure athletic competition, but it wouldn't have the same overall effect and appeal.

Are uniforms valuable? Unbelievably so. Your cleaning (just like the halfback's playing) can be perfect, but if you perform in sweaty, wrinkled, mismatched garments, you attract no attention and give no positive message.

Uniforms lend authority. What if, while going home today, you hear a siren and see a red light behind you and you're pulled over by an officer of the law. Fear grips your stomach, but when you look out the window at the policeman standing there you see he's wearing flowered swim trunks, a battered straw hat, a surfing t-shirt and rubber thongs. What is your reaction? Eighty percent of the fear disappears! How would we recognize a fireman without his helmet and boots, carpenter without his tool belt, a mail carrier without his light blues and bag? Just think for a minute how much impact the "uniform" has on a doctor, judge, soldier, dancer, just about any professional. It's the one thing that instantly projects competence and identifies them.

I would never appear on any job, even a volunteer neighborhood project, without my uniform. It makes me the leader, the authority of the job. You as a professional cleaner need this advantage as much as any professional. Yet the majority of cleaning people work without any kind of a uniform!

Uniforms aren't an attempt at regimentation; they're a positive image builder. Uniforms are an inexpensive way to give identity and recognition, even to the shyest or meekest member of your cleaning crew. Cleaning isn't a private job, it's a public job, and anything that can be done to arouse public awareness of it—DO IT! Uniforms don't have to be complicated, but they should be comfortable to wear and easy to clean and get in and out of. We use a polo shirt with company logo on the front and back, and the name of the employee on the front. Uniforms offer other advantages to the motivation and image-building of your cleaning crews:

• They identify who you are so people don't worry that you might be a rapist or mugger.

• They help keep people productive and honest. When everyone knows who you are and what you're doing, it's hard to be a slacker.

• Security: Uniforms make it immediately clear that you're a cleaner, not a sneak thief or burglar. Whether they're inside or even outside tromping garbage, it'll save your crews many police raids and questions.

In some cases t-shirts are okay, and they're certainly better than nothing. But, there are only a few people who have the build to look good in a t-shirt. If someone is a little overweight, or too thin, they look like a stuffed animal or a scarecrow.

Special Occasion Uniforms

T-shirts or sweatshirts for company picnics or meetings or special events, can be made up cheaper than you think. It costs around $50 for the setup screen plus the cost of the shirts. A t-shirt store can imprint a special message or design for any occasion. Here are some of the ones we made up for the students in a Facility Care

Course. You might only use them officially once or twice, but they last for years to wear at home, and they don't cost any more than the average meal. And they'll give a lasting image and rousing memory.

Put a Name with the Face

Although a uniform will identify what you do, it doesn't always tell the most important thing—who you are! Remember that one of the most important parts of improving image is getting others to recognize you and your crew as human beings, as individuals. Name tags give others the one thing that really makes you a living, breathing person to them—your name! Without a name on the uniform you are only "Hey, buddy," or "Hey, boy," or "Uh, Mister (or Ma'am), would you clean this?" After they glance at the tag a time or two, they'll come to know you. And knowing you will make a real difference in how they treat you—you'll be surprised how conscious they'll become of treating the facility better, too—making your job easier.

If possible, have a name patch sewn on the uniform. This way you'll avoid losing the pin-on kind that gets raked off when you're dumping the trash.

Always have name tags, too, at dinners, socials, assemblies, and other events—coming up with some clever ones is sure fun. I used the one at the right at 70 seminars across the U.S. for the Bell System. All the big wheel

managers wore them with pride. Where the little squeegee is, I pinned on a real gold-plated squeegee lapel pin (it didn't cost much and was a nice little gift they could carry home with them after the seminar).

This name tag told a story about us and our profession. People instantly warmed up to me and the seminar when they read the tags. I heard comments throughout the hotel at lunch time, it was a wonderful attention getter.

At our Varsity cleaning convention in Denver another time, the hosting manager made clever toilet seat name tags. You had to lift the lid to see the name. It was a lot of fun and a great conversation starter. The entire hotel—guests and staff alike—sure knew what we did for a living.

You've seen a few of our ideas now (you can order some of these items, see page 76), and I know that you and your staff will be able to come up with your own eye-stoppers.

Give Them Some Space

Most of the time when it comes to this we say "I love you but I have no space for you." While others who have minor responsibility in a building have scores of often wasted square feet, the janitors generally get the leftover cubbyholes, abandoned vaults, waterheater closets, old elevator shafts, and little caves under staircases. These things are poorly located and poorly ventilated and must be shared with pipes, telephone equipment and anything that the other departments want to dump in them.

It's hard to feel good about yourself and your job if your workplace is cramped, inconvenient, and unattractive. Maybe you can't change the size of the janitor closet now, but perhaps you can find some space somewhere else and move some of the storage to that room so that the janitor closet can be used by the janitors instead of serving as a catch-all storage shed. Space to call your own motivates and gives the

message that the cleaning crew is important to the business team. Words alone don't say it, but deeds DO!

Identify a Leader

There are bosses, supervisors, managers, and owners of operations, but often in the whole mainstream of management, there is no one for the janitors to identify and communicate with. Who is it that they trust to always listen to them and look out for them? Somewhere in your group of service people is someone who is trusted, who will speak for others and speak with them. Ask your people now who in the organization they think could represent them—someone who they can confide in and look up to.

Give your cleaning people a leader they trust and see that he or she is listened to by you... and watch production soar!

Stop Scrimping on Tools and Supplies– It's Costing You

It has always amazed me that when the copy machine in the central office is performing at anything less than 100%, salespeople and consultants are rushed in to repair or replace it. In the very same building, I'll give you odds that a lot more time and money is being lost on inadequate tools and equipment for the maintenance department, and no one in management is even aware of it. Tools, supplies, in and equipment generally run about 6% of the gross cleaning dollars. Labor runs about 65%. Yet in an attempt to cut costs, companies invariably will try every imaginable method of cutting the cost of cleaning supplies and equipment. They postpone buying needed buffers and vacuums, put off repairs, use frozen or damaged chemicals, all sincerely trying to save a buck.

It's ironic, because even if that effort succeeds and they do reduce their total supply costs by say 30%, they've only saved 2% of the maintenance dollars. And at the same time they're wasting about a third of their much larger labor costs by trying to limp along with poor equipment and supplies. Which ends up a net loss in operation efficiency of 20%... so you can see it will cost you rather than pay to scrimp on tools and supplies. Good tools and equipment don't guarantee a good job, but they certainly lessen the burden for the cleaning people. Good equipment is a motivator.

How many of your other employees have to make do with outdated, inefficient equipment? They'd revolt if they still had to function with manual typewriters, full key adding machines, or carbon paper copies. All of these will still do the job, but.... How do you think the cleaning people feel trying to get by with the obsolete models and the leftovers? Upgrading your supplies and equipment won't just improve morale, it'll up your cleaning productivity and quality 10 or 15%. This is one way that maintenance contractors are beating in-house operations. They keep up with the fastest and the best equipment because it's cheaper in the long run. "Quality" chemicals may be a little more expensive, but they work a lot better, keep your crews happier, and cut labor costs considerably. Better equipment and supplies will also reduce expensive damage to the buildings and surfaces being cleaned.

Find a service-oriented supplier dealing in good products, and work with them to keep the best materials and equipment at your disposal. They want your business and will give you a price only a few cents different than bidding.

Let the people using the stuff have a voice in choosing it (have them attend the pre-budget meeting). They'll probably pick less expensive and better stuff than you. They know what works. Nothing is worse than someone else picking out your tools and supplies and saying "Here, now go to work."

Owning up to your cleaning-supply mistakes will do a lot to encourage your cleaners, too. For years I've watched purchasing agents lay in cases of window cleaner that streaks—the janitors hate it, but purchasing says, "You've got to use it up before buying any new." What a de-motivator it is to know you are stuck with junk. Dump your cleaning garbage! Forcing people to use it will cost, not save.

Take advantage of the circle of pride: a janitor taking pride in himself, will take pride in his work, will take pride in his company, will take pride in his equipment. Good, sharp, efficient equipment will motivate cleaners to take better care of the equipment.

Go Watch Them Work

Watch them on the job, like people on the sidewalk watch the cranes and the contractors do their jobs. Most cleaners are proud to be expert with a spray bottle or buffer and yet for the most part, who cares? Watch and ask questions for ten minutes or so, once in a while. It'll save you ten hours of puffed-up praise later on!

Whenever possible, too, arrange for yourself or one of your cleaning supervisors to work right with your employees on the job. There are several good reasons for this:

1. It builds respect, loyalty and trust, and you can get to know them better.
2. You can train them while you yourself are in a productive, money-making situation.
3. You can evaluate their performance firsthand and know who will be the best for promotion and future upward moves. No one else can tell you this.

Work with and around and for them, while you're with them show them that you're willing to do the dirtiest and toughest jobs, too.

Listen

Janitors are pretty smart and are well worth listening to. In one school, for example, some girls blotted their lipstick in the bathroom by kissing the mirror. The janitors, of course, couldn't get it off easily and mentioned it to the principal, who immediately got on the school intercom and announced, "We will not kiss the mirrors in the school anymore." Well you know what that said in reality, "The greatest new sensual thrill is kissing restroom mirrors."

Every girl began kissing the mirrors, it became a fad. The principal put guards in the restroom, the guards began kissing the mirrors. Like many high school fads it got out of hand and soon a couple of students were up for expulsion over mirror kissing.

Then one morning, the oldest, wisest janitor walked into the board meeting and suggested that if he had just five minutes at the next assembly, he could iron out the mirror kissing problem. He was granted the privilege and he walked out on the stage before a full auditorium with a miniature toilet under his arm and in the other hand a bowl swab. Students observed and listened in guilty silence as the old janitor said, "Hey, we're the guys who clean your restrooms, we spend hours on them every day and do a good job and you abuse them. To show you how hard we work I'd like to do a demonstration of how we clean."

He set the toilet down, whipped the swab around the bowl and said, "First, we thoroughly clean the inside of the toilets," pulling the swab out he said, "right after the toilets are done, we do the mirrors," and he whisked the swab across his imaginary mirror. The audience gasped, and all mirror kissing stopped from that moment on.

Listen, some wise old—and young—janitors will educate you. Ask for opinions from your cleaning people. Ask them to participate and help solve a problem or two. Invite them to meetings concerning the next major building or remodeling project. Call the "cleaners" in and show them the plans and ask them to suggest any-thing that might make it easier to clean. Have a mattress handy (because at least one of them will faint in disbelief). And after you hear their suggestions at least one of you will faint when you realize the great stuff you've been missing.

Knowing that our opinions count, and are taken seriously, motivates us all.

Involve Them

Involve your people in the day-to-day decisions about their work, too. Involve them in choosing the crew for an assignment and they will feel responsible to produce. Let them present their own complaints to the mediator instead of going through five others. Let them figure out their schedules, so that if they want to double things up, or put in some late hours in exchange for some longer weekend privileges, they can do it, as long as they deliver. I promise that you'll get higher production and motivated people.

Feeling that you have some control over your destiny gives you confidence and motivation to exceed the expected performance.

Make Sure They Attend Important Meetings Related to Their Work

It's terribly important to have the supervisor or lead person sit in on meetings to hear the plans, complaints, praises, and needs of the tenants as well as the cleaners. Often the supervisor of maintenance (who is generally the overall controller of utilities, safety, energy, and scheduling for a facility) is never invited to these meetings. All the needs and news are reported to her or him secondhand, seldom in the spirit originally intended. Literally hundreds of problems can be solved if a representative from the cleaning staff attends the meeting—and that may

> Memo
>
> To: Mrs. Franklin, Environmental Services
>
> From: Allen Green, Operations Mgr.
>
> RE: Building Policy Meeting
>
> The regional meeting will be held a week from Tuesday, October 15th, 7 to 9 pm at the Center Street office building conference room. You or a volunteer representative from your department are invited to attend. Please let me know the name of the attendee by Monday, October 14th.
>
> Thank you

not always mean the boss. When crew members attend, they feel good about your confidence and do a great job.

From time to time, ask your cleaning people to "dress up" and attend a big conference or meeting with the executives. You should have a "cleaner" there anyway to police up spills, move tables, etc. This is a rare and appreciated assignment, even once a year or every other year—they will never forget!

Actions Speak Louder Than Words

The public and you as management constantly send messages to the janitors without saying a word. You can be totally polite, talk to the custodial staff nicely, and even pay them well and still be Mr. or Ms. Putdown on the Hoof. Your actions say very plainly what you really think of them. I've attended a lot of "motivational" events, for example, that end up talking down to the cleaning people.

I'm sure you know what I'm referring to—maybe you're guilty of it: The cleaning people are holding a meeting, special training session, or maybe even a seminar. Upper management decides it would be a great idea to put in an appearance, give the cleaning people a shot in the arm, emphasize their importance to the team. The meeting starts and the "big wheel" (the president or other top official) is ushered in and introduced. He or she then gives the old familiar speech, "You people are valuable to our organization, we can't get along without you..." Or he steps in and shakes a few hands and nods and fidgets around for a few minutes. Then he hurries out of the room to grab a leisurely cup of coffee in the lounge with his fellow executives.

This kind of behavior lets the janitors know what the people upstairs really think: that their little meeting isn't quite important enough for management to sit in on. It tells them that no one in the upper echelon is really interested in their jobs. Instances like these do more to destroy janitor morale than anything else.

If the janitors were truly valuable, if he couldn't get along without them, then wouldn't the speaker stay for at least part of the session, share in some of the programs, get to know them, or have lunch or coffee with them? Wouldn't he show some courtesy by listening to what the main speaker has to say or one of the custodial presentations? Everyone hates the "spot" speaker—short, insincere attempts like this to build image end up actually undermining employee relations.

Management would be more appreciated—and they'd get more credit—if they provided a nice snack for the break and a note on the table saying, "Thank you, ladies and gentle-men, for a good job done over and over again. Although we never see you, we know from our clean building that you've been here. Thanks from the head office. Signed, the Boss."

We don't need to be told we're important, but to be shown we're important, and **treated** like we're important. We're constantly told how important we are, but seldom shown. The president of a huge facility will give a tear-jerking speech on how it can't run without the maintenance staff, and twenty minutes later veto the purchase of a $300 machine that would enable them to make much more efficient use of their personnel.

If the accounting department needs a $60,000 computer to help with payroll—bang, they'll get it! But ask for $150 worth of better toilet paper holders to prevent complaints and vandalism and you can't even get anyone's attention.

I was called to give a seminar training session to the custodial crew, supervisors, and managers of one of our country's largest, most prestigious

There **is** a person in there, a real, live, sensitive human being who wants love, praise, and appreciation.

firms. They led me to the place for the presentation, one side of a noisy cafeteria, where we could "set up chairs and turn down the elevator music a little." I asked the manager about using the luxurious, full-size, plush conference room upstairs (which the group vacuumed and maintained), and the manager about passed out.

"Oh that's for our scientists and executives. Do you realize we have $200,000 in tables, chairs and audio visual equipment in there?"

"Who knows the executive suites better than those who clean them?", I replied. "I find it strange that we are worthy to go in and clean it, entrusted with the keys, access and security, yet we can't sit in there and hold a seminar. You're trying to convince the custodians they're as important as every worker in the plant but you give them the pigsty to meet in. Giving them the best room in the house will say more about your appreciation level than anything you can say in the meeting."

A light came on in the manager's face and he said, "Man, you're right. They actually would take better care of the room than the scientists and executives."

So use it we did, and the custodians were in awe and got the message loud and clear: YOU ARE WORTHWHILE!

What Are Some of the Other Things We Do That Quietly Undermine Our Cleaners?

• Forgetting to include them with the "other" people: I did a "Begin the Year" in-service session for the whole staff (bus drivers, teachers, cooks, administrators, librarians) at one school. And guess who wasn't invited? I asked the superintendent right on the spot, "Where are your custodians?" His face was deservedly red for the rest of the meeting—the people most directly involved with school security, safety, sanitation, utility use, and school PR they had forgotten to invite. **Lots of you**, even those directly in charge of custodial departments, **forget to invite them!**

• Ignoring their opinions on things. Most janitors are actually better organizers than those in the MBA ranks; they know how to get things done. Even if you don't always end up using them, ask for their opinions and consider them. (See page 22.)

• Always giving them the last choice (or no choice) of break and vacation times.

• Giving them the worst locations imaginable for their janitor closets, poor parking places, poor seating in assemblies. The janitors always get the last and the least... space assignment like this is a silent putdown. (See page 20.)

• Thankless sheep stealing (or taking all the sharp people out of the janitorial ranks), which in effect says "You are too smart to be a cleaner, to remain here with the dummies of the operation!" Make any transfers a move "up" instead of a move "out." How do you suppose the remaining people feel, having someone taken away time after time, because they're so good? This tells them that **they** are no good, which isn't the least bit upgrading or motivating. At least thank and credit the cleaning department for molding you some big-league players—**give the department the credit**, all of it. They can use it better than anyone else.

Openly Support Your Janitor When He or She is Right

Maintenance people are vulnerable to criticism: furnaces quit, doors jam, baskets don't get emptied, and thousands of other things go wrong. No one says a word about the 99 days the air conditioning was perfect or the floors or drapes were beautiful, but let a small problem develop and management and tenants alike will all be whining at the service folks. Often these things are not the fault of the cleaning people. It only takes a manager sticking up for his staff once or twice before you'll notice them giving their "all" on the job.

Many times when an occasion arises that the cleaning staff is erroneously blamed for something, we let it go and miss a great motivational opportunity.

So side with them publicly— employees expect their supervisors to stand up for them, but when the big boss does, everyone takes notice, especially the ones being defended.

Getting Some Good Press For Our Honesty

All of us have seen and even received headlines like these:

"Janitor Finds Diamond Bracelet"
"Janitor Returns Lost $50 Bill"
"Janitor Delivers Missing Coat"

My company receives letters daily from customers praising our janitors for acts of honesty. They surely perform twice the number we hear about and it's a shame we don't make the most of it. It's not the fault of the appreciative recipient of the lost item that they don't know the name of the benevolent janitor—that's where we can help. Usually the found item is locked up in the closet or handed over to the receptionist or boss. The one who lost it and gets it back seldom knows who and what the circumstances of the return were. It's a heartwarming experience to have a lost item returned to you; it makes you feel good inside and it makes you feel good about the person who did the good deed, too. But as we all know credit is seldom given where credit is due. Nine times out of ten, it's the janitor who sees that items are returned. We're not looking for a reward, but a simple acknowledgment can be a valuable public relations tool.

An easy way to accomplish this is to have a *dazzling lost and found department.* Simply attach a clever tag like this to the returned item, person-

Don Aslett, World's #1 Cleaning Expert

We're glad you got your lost item back. As professionals in maintenance, we constantly find items such as eyeglasses, coats, pills, books—why, we've even found $125,000 cash in a wastebasket! We are the most trusted people in society. We report and turn in found items immediately, but there is one thing that will help both you and I...

Put your name on your possessions!

Thanks!

Don Aslett Inc • PO Box 700 • Pocatello ID 83204 • 208-232-3535

RECEIPT OF RETURN

I received my _____ on _____ Signed _____

This item: _____
was found by: _____
Where: _____
When: Date _____ Time _____
Turned in to: _____

26

ally signed by the finder, and it will spread trust, good feelings and comradeship between the building users and cleaners like wildfire. The receiver is relieved to have the item returned, but they're also delighted to know that a real human, with a name and feelings and concern (not just a faceless janitor) went to some trouble to return it.

This brings a flood of respect to the cleaning profession and the cleaners. The tags also stave off unwarranted accusations of theft.

Keep a dozen or so in each cleaning closet. It's an inexpensive way to build janitor/tenant bonds in your building. "Found" tags are a must, make your own or order them from my company (see page 76).

Have Them Teach Classes

Your cleaners are professionals. They get paid for performing a service. Few of them realize that the knowledge and skill they possess is needed and wanted by many. Who's teaching today's kids and new families how to clean? It's not Mom anymore. And would you let TV do it? Holding cleaning classes for the tenants, the public or invited groups, at the office during the day or in the evening and asking your cleaners to teach the segments on floors or windows will do more for their self-esteem than five years' worth of praise and nickel-and-dime raises.

Teaching students— children or adults— how we clean actually commits us to better performance. The very fact that other people are showing an interest in what we do makes us feel good and intensifies our identification with our profession. It forces us to be sharp and often, to bone up on things. It also introduces us to the people in the building, office, or school as another human being, not a mop-wielding robot.

The opportunities for involving your janitors in outside speaking assignments don't stop there. **Everyone** is interested in cleaning demonstrations. Speaking, lecturing, or teaching on cleaning in your local area is an outstanding public relations and motivational opportunity. Junior high and high schools, colleges, church groups, and senior centers are all looking for people to give them some "outside spark." This is an opportunity to change lives for the better as well as to raise the visibility and image of cleaning professionals. Contact your local council on aging, the County Extension office, schools, and clubs and tell them that you have cleaners available to speak on cleaning. They will call you! Here are some examples of the possibilities:

College: Parks and Recreation and business classes always have sessions on "Should you contract the cleaning or do it yourself?"

High school: Career classes are always looking for someone to come in and tell them about our business. Your staff can hustle up some future workers while they entertain and teach. Home economics classes love to hear about faster and better professional cleaning methods and equipment.

Grade School: How about a "Cleaning Assembly" to teach and motivate youngsters to "mess less" and help keep things clean at home and school?

Women's clubs and church groups: Are dying for professional information about cleaning techniques and how to streamline cleaning efforts.

These assignments do great things for your staff. They sharpen skills and improve self-esteem, as well as our public image.

Create a Cleaning Information Center

Have you ever heard of a resource room for the janitors? Their own library? That's what I thought. But what is more practical? Your cleaning staff is not only responsible for the care and maintenance of entire buildings and all of their contents, it controls most of the security in those buildings, most of the utilities, most of the safety programs, and has considerable influence on public relations. Who needs reference books, informational videos, and technical manuals more than the maintenance department? The majority of your crew has probably never even read a cleaning publication of any kind. They probably don't even know there are professional cleaner's magazines, videotapes and other materials available. A resource center is also an effective motivator because it establishes identity.

It doesn't have to be a big place, a 5' x 4' space would do. Make the library available to your clients as well as to your people. There are always students who need reference material, and others in the building who would be very interested in information on how to clean better and faster. If your cleaners and your tenants get their hands on good material it will actually help them do their jobs better, faster and cheaper. They'll automatically come to you and your company for help and give you more attention, respect, and business.

You probably know of several books on cleaning and may have a good start for your library. Following is a good starter list of books and other publications I subscribe to. Investing a couple hundred dollars in your own library will easily save you much more than that in waste, error, and inefficiency.

Your library can start out as one shelf. Just save and collect all the good information that comes across your desk and you'll be adding shelves every year.

You can also put together your own manuals, illustrated instructions, training publications, etc. For such a vast profession we have an amazingly small amount of literature—books and other printed information available. Try your hand at it,

28

There are many fine books out there by all sorts of experts—here are some good ones by "America's #1 Cleaning Expert."

Books:
- *The Professional Cleaner's Personal Handbook*
- *Cleaning Up for a Living*
- *Check Up: How to Achieve Quality Control*
- *How to Upgrade & Motivate Your Cleaning Crews*
- *Don Aslett's Stainbuster's Bible*
- *Is There Life After Housework?*
- *The Cleaning Encyclopedia*
- *Don Aslett's Clean in a Minute*
- *Painting Without Fainting*
- *Wood Floor Care*
- *Pet Clean-Up Made Easy*
- *Who Says It's a Woman's Job to Clean?*
- *Make Your House Do the Housework*
- *Clutter's Last Stand*
- *For Packrats Only*
- *Clutter Free! Finally & Forever*
- *The Office Clutter Cure*
- *Lose 200 Lbs. This Weekend*
- *How to be #1 With Your Boss*
- *Everything I Needed to Know About Business I Learned in the Barnyard*
- *Is There a Speech Inside You?*

Videos:
- *Is There Life After Housework?*
- *Clean in a Minute*

Periodicals:
American Window Cleaner
  510-222-7080
Cleanfax Magazine
  614-587-1393
Cleaning Management
  518-783-1281
Executive Housekeeping Today
  (Published by National Executive Housekeepers Association, Inc.)
  614-895-7166
Installation & Cleaning Specialist
  818-345-3550
Maintenance Executive
  319-364-6167
Maintenance Supplies
  516-845-2700
Services (Published by Building Service Contractors Association)
  703-359-7090

All of these books and videos are available from my office. There is an order form in the back of this book.

Send me a postcard with your name and address for a free catalog.

Don Aslett
PO Box 700
Pocatello, ID 83204

you have a wealth of knowledge in your head and in your staff that many others could benefit from. Consult with a local quick printer, or one of the specialized book printers, for guidance on doing this attractively and inexpensively in the quantities you think you need.

Make Better Use of Bulletin Boards

Bulletin boards in most buildings are buried under waste paper and JUNK. Most of what's on there is outdated, unkempt or of little significance. Have you ever seen anything about cleaning or building maintenance (except for safety) on those boards? Start this very week to post cleaning information and pictures and I'll bet you'll get more reaction and positive comments than you can imagine. How about posting cleaning schedules so that everyone in the building knows when their carpet and floor will be done? What a PR move that would be. It not only advertises the activities of the cleaning crew, it makes each tenant involved and important. You can also make a clever cleaning bulletin board in one corner of the main board and post cleaning information, news about the cleaning crew, and pass along helpful information about home cleaning.

Get It on Film!

Here is a great way to say "I care" that costs very little, and automatically doubles the benefit of any company activity or event.

A wise old sage once told me there are two things people will never forget you for: 1. if you visit them when they're sick or in the hospital and 2. if you give them a nice picture of themselves or their family. His counsel has proven true time and again.

I've found that sending a $10 video copy of a training session, motivational event, or an interesting company happening to a satellite office can sometimes do more good than making a personal visit which would cost hundreds or thousands of dollars.

Never let an event or gathering go without recording it on video tape or film. People never tire of seeing themselves, and they're always interested in seeing candid shots. Film is cheap, so take plenty of pictures. If you don't have picture taking capabilities among your staff (which is hard to imagine), you could invite a camera-happy friend or family member for the purpose. And of course there are always inexpensive professionals who will come and take pictures for you.

Likewise, there's hardly a one of us who doesn't have access to a video system—they're cheap to rent, and tapes cost less than $5. You also wouldn't have any problem finding a real video enthusiast in your ranks who'll come and film everything for you.

Be sure your "photographer" takes color prints (to pass around and pin up) as well as black and white prints that will reproduce better in your newsletter. Don't forget slides, too, if the event will make a good picture story, slide show, or crowd pleaser.

WHAT TO DO WITH THE PICTURES

Once you have those pictures, have extra copies made and pass them around and use them forever.

Post them: Posting pictures of an event or gathering will at least double everyone's enjoyment, enthusiasm, and recollection of it. Pick out the best shots and post them in the halls, lunch-room, etc. A picture pin-up says "You're important," "We had a great time, didn't we?," "We're proud and we're showing you off!" It also lets people see that the cleaning department is very much alive and active.

Enlargements: For those exceptional pictures, it only costs a few dollars to have them enlarged and present them as a gift or award.

Make a slide show: Anyone can make a good slide show for the next company meeting with a few clever lines and a little collection of slides.

OLD-TIME PHOTOS

A fun event that's great for a group. One time my own company, for example, took a bunch of antique cleaning equipment and some early-1900s clothes and had a studio camera set up—just like at the fair. Then we photographed groups of our employees dressed in old-time garb, posing with the antiques. After the event, we mailed the brown-tone pictures out (a $3 investment on our part) to every participant and they were ecstatic. Most of those pictures are still proudly hanging on office walls today.

You can look in the Yellow Pages to find photographers who offer "old-time" and other specialty photo services—they'll come right to your place with all the gear and trappings and then you can just let the old times roll. If it's an important event and you have any doubts about the quality of your in-house photographer, call a professional. They'll give you a good job at a fair price.

Pictures are one more way to weld us together with our employees and give visibility and meaning to our profession.

Do Something for Them When They're Down and Out

We've all had or known employees, friends, or even family who are just plain difficult to "get to." They might be aloof and unresponsive to offers of kindness, in other words, they need help but are next to impossible to help. You invite them, and they decline; you put other people to work with them, and they withdraw. These, "the difficult" to upgrade and motivate, are the ones who need it the most. This type of person very often filters down to the maintenance department, and once there, are generally ignored and it's believed they like it that way. Yet the poor production and unhappiness they so often show is an indication they haven't found the answer.

No matter how independent, self-reliant, or reserved we are, there comes a time, in serious illness or injury, when our confidence is truly shaken. We feel down and discouraged, totally vulnerable. We may even be battling all manner of morbid thoughts. This is the time when any one of us really welcomes attention, help, concern, and encouragement. If you can seize that moment, you'll capture love and loyalty and instill self-worth. A sick or injured person will never forget who visited them when they were sick, or in deep sadness over a death in the family.

I cut the tendons in my finger once and had to be instantly hospitalized for surgery. At the time we had a contract for Bell System and that night as I lay in the hospital with a giant cast on my arm who should walk in, but Les Hodge, the biggest, toughest, most feared telephone boss in the state. He came with his wife and they wanted to know how I was doing and offered to help with anything I might need two hands for. They stayed for ten minutes and left. I was loyal to him to the death from then on. Those ten simple minutes at a crucial time

for me meant more than candy, flowers, or any raise or praise ever could have.

Every single one of us has a turn at "down time"—due to physical or mental problems or family setbacks, so don't miss the opportunity, just pay a visit or even make a phone call if there's no other choice. And when the crew gets the word you visited one of them, it's almost as if you visited them all.

Consider also that when it comes to a grave illness or death in the immediate family, expenses are a burden added to grief. Family members come to the house, stay, eat, and often drain the budget. If taste and circumstances permit, money really helps here.

When I got news that one of my former Sun Valley office managers, who had worked for us for six years, passed away, I knew that the family already faced a lot of bills from the extended illness. So I sent a cashier's check for $500 as a token to help out. When word got around (secretaries tell all) that "the boss" still helps and loves past employees, my current crew was all the better for it. If you do send money, always send a cashier's check, so they have to use it.

Struggling times also mean conflicts with work schedules. The minute you hear of a problem, before it has a chance to mess up the routine and weigh heavily on the employee's mind, sit down, express genuine concern, and talk about what it might mean in terms of needed time off. If you bring it up and help lay out a solution, this will alleviate pressure on the employee and reduce fears, as well as keep you covered.

Involve Family

When people ask about your profession, do you suspect that your spouse would rather tell them you're a college professor or computer programmer? Have your kids ever had a hard time telling their friends you're a custodian or a janitorial-supply salesman?

Cleaning people's spouses and children often have a hard time understanding how anyone could choose janitoring as a life's work. They have a hard time admitting to others that a member of the family is also a member of the cleaning society. It's important to involve your employees' family members as much as possible so that they understand this is a bona fide profession we're engaged in.

One time we hired a supervisor who used to be a department manager in a large company. His wife just couldn't accept his new position—a demotion, a loss of status from her point of view—and rather than encourage and support him, she found every occasion to nag and voice her dissatisfaction. At the first company function she attended, she was stunned to find out that her husband looked very much at home in the midst of our sharp and efficient businesspeople. After seeing the enthusiasm of others for their jobs and the degree of professionalism they all displayed, she was a changed woman.

And as her attitude turned around, her husband's work took an obvious upswing. Give the family a chance to find out first hand how many good people are in the business. They'll also begin to see that there's a real source of pride in being a cleaner. The stigma at home will disappear—there'll be less nagging, and more bragging. As in any profession, when cleaning people are supported at home, their work is improved.

SOME GOOD WAYS TO INVOLVE FAMILY

• **Family Occasions:** If you watch and listen, there are all sorts of things going on with employees' families—Little League, football, soccer, musical events, weddings, engagements, hospitalizations, reunions, and more. An acknowledgment from you of their special occasion will mean a lot.

Recognizing marriage anniversaries is a nice touch, too, something few bosses are savvy enough to do.

Think of how you feel when someone does something nice for your kids or family. You're grateful and impressed and deeply appreciative of the act. We may even enjoy the attention given to our family more than that given directly to us. A $100 scholarship given at graduation to one of your janitor's daughters could be the best $100 you'll ever spend. Even if you spend $500, I know you'll get more than that back in goodwill and production out of the employee and their positive influence on others.

• **Remember to Double Everything:** Dinner or lunch certificates given as awards, ball game tickets, trips and all, it costs only a little more to include the custodian's spouse or date or one of the kids in a fun or special occasion. Thanks to who? The boss, the cleaning department—they love it and the second ticket recipient **never** forgets it!

• **Go to Their Homes:** This is especially important because few people recognize the janitor as more than a fixture or see their home as more than a janitor closet. As the leader, just once or twice go home with them, stop by their house on a day off. Look at the son's room, the garden, the new remodeling job, etc. I promise it will do both of you more good than all the new incentive programs in the world.

• **Send Professional Publications and Company News, etc., to Their Homes:** Don't just hand things like this out at work and ask the employees to share them with their families. You'd be surprised how many parents figure their kids aren't interested in mom or dad's "work," but many kids will devour it if given a chance.

• **Make Sure the Maintenance Department is Included:** in the rest of the company's family programs, like picnics, softball games, scholarships, etc. Everyone forgets to invite the janitors, but as the leader it's your responsibility to see that they and their families aren't forgotten. In turn you and your company's welfare will be in their minds for a long, long time.

• **Schedule Your Own Janitorial Special Events (see Chapter 10):** And be sure to invite the family.

We especially like to bring in and involve children in our various company events. We run poster and cleaning slogan contests, slide shows, talent shows, etc., for them.

If you involve a person's family in your operation, you make pride in the job a family affair. What better motivational step can you make?

Last, Let Them Have Some Glory

Nobody ever passes on cleaning related news or accomplishments, or lets the cleaning people run touchdowns. I remember we had a contract to furnish decorated Christmas trees at the Sun Valley resort and an order came through to take a tree to Steve McQueen's room. Naturally all the managers wanted the honor. Instead I asked a shy young woman on the day shift if she would like to deliver the tree—of course she did. And Steve lifted her up to put the star on top. Was that ever job motivation!

5 Complaints:

The Pro Cleaner's #1 Confidence Killer

Remember those stores that had a complaint department? If we did that in the cleaning business, it would be our largest department! It's indigenous to the industry: people take the positive for granted and report only the negative. Nine times out of ten if you walk up to the building manager, client, or a tenant and ask how the cleaning is, regardless of its condition they'll make a negative or critical comment. If you indiscriminately ask how the cleaning is, people think you're looking to them to find problems and soon they'll hoard up little bits of complaints so they'll have something to tell you.

Because we cleaners hear more complaints than we do compliments, we gradually develop a negativism ourselves toward the public we clean for, and end up constantly complaining about their complaints. The irony of this situation is that the complaints end up getting all the attention while the compliments get very little, if any, mileage.

To help change this situation, when you talk to a tenant or client, don't ask how the cleaning is. Instead, ask for specific things they like about the condition of the building—or don't ask at all. You really don't need to seek out critics.

The positive reinforcement you'll get as a result if you try this different tack will have a wonderful effect on your cleaners. And if we take the time to **respond** to compliments, people will give us more compliments, instead of complaining! In fact, they'll be too busy complimenting us to have time to complain!

From Complaints to Compliments

Complaint/compliment—such similar words with entirely opposite meanings. Yet they can be of almost equal value when it comes to upgrading and motivating. There will always be complaints because remember, we're in a business that takes the positive for granted and reports the negative. Complaints can actually be turned into compliments, if you handle them right. But what usually happens? Well, because every complaint to a cleaning person is from someone higher up, he or she feels that to refute or refuse a complaint is flush-yourself-down-the-toilet suicide. So the usual procedure is to shut up, redo it, and forget it.

This pattern cuts you out of one of the real rewards of our profession—a chance to have meaningful personal contact with people. A maintenance complaint is never to a person; it's to an institution, that anonymous "they." Many a fun and fact-filled experience (and new friend) comes from answering a complaint in person. So seek out the complainer—whether it was fair or not is immaterial—you'll make out fine either way. Meeting people may be the skill maintenance

people most often lack. But a complaint is an invitation to "Come and see me"—twice! Once to get the details and take care of the problem—the second time to see if everything is all right (which you're sure of before you drop by). If you do this right you will undoubtedly pick up the other word: compliment, for handling it. Once you meet face to face, you and your complainer will never look at each other again quite the same way, because you'll realize that you're both human beings capable of making mistakes.

The minute you feel a complainer is an enemy, any motivational or upgrading opportunity is gone, and it becomes strictly an obligation to fulfill. Personal contact is the only reward we have in cleaning; it lasts even though our work doesn't. After one or two visits they'll never want to complain and you will do work to merit that—they will be proud they met you and you won't be carrying a grudge.

From today on, start collecting all the written complaints and compliments that come your way. Go to the copy machine and shrink the complaints down and enlarge the compliments and hang them side by side on the bulletin board. Under the compliments write, "Great job, gang… MORE!" and sign your name. Under the complaints, don't point any fingers, just write, "How can we fix this so we can move this to the compliment side?" or "What could we do next time to help avoid this?" Start giving your clients a chance to give some compliments. And use the complaints you do get to start a positive exchange with your staff.

Is it a Complaint or a Human Relations Conflict?

A long time ago I learned that 95% of the complaints we receive aren't for a poorly done job, but are public relations problems—a conflict between people, not really about the work.

When it comes to training, cleaners are often told how, where, and when to clean, but rarely anything about how to effectively interact with the people we're cleaning for. Yet cleaning is a very personal thing. We're invading another person's space, touching their things, removing their dirt—we need to know how to get along with our clients, not just how to strip their floors.

5 Common Reasons for Friction Between Clients and Cleaners (and what to do about them)

1 **Everyone is an expert:** Everyone is an expert in the job we happen to do, at least they think they are. Everyone you clean for, even the most incredible messmaker, thinks he knows your job better than you and will go out of his way to make that clear to you. These "experts" make rash statements and judgments about the cleaning process or the cleanliness level, even if they don't know a thing about the schedules, the conditions, the contract, the hours, or even the duties you're supposed to be performing.

2 **Invisibility factor:** Very seldom is much of the work that a custodian does seen by the public. They rarely see him or her, and most of the work we cleaners do only lasts for a few hours in the morning. The public doesn't relate the job or the work to any actual person. That's why the boss resents paying for it and people complain, "Those janitors never do anything." (The same office is full of people who have titles, positions, and degrees but never really do anything and no one gives them a second glance or thought.)

See Chapter 4 for ways to counter invisibility.

3 **Jealous of the Janitor:** Yes, it exists! No one really wants to be a janitor, but everyone wants the job—not for themselves, of course, but so some family member can do it part time and make extra money. The average worker feels that janitors are overpaid and underworked. "They get $600 a month for this building… and you never see them." I'm always amazed how everyone in the building knows what the janitors are getting paid, yet don't have a clue what they are doing when they work or what risks they take.

4 **The "Richer Than Me" Syndrome:** The janitor is used as a base judgement for all pay scales. Look in any major paper. They'll compare the judges, the secretaries, the health officers, all the services and trades, and even the administration to the janitor. There's nothing people hate worse than the thought that the janitor might make more than they do. I've got hundreds of friends and acquaintances who worry night and day about what I make as a cleaner. They equate a few exceptionally successful people in the profession with all (which is about as logical as "If one lawyer is dishonest, they all must be!"). To defuse this one I learned (and it worked) to wear my white or work uniform most of the time even to the office, and my work boots. It says I'm the worker and the servant and the big clients love that, to see me working on a job with a pick and shovel just pleases them beyond words. Even today I make sure they're pleased—they see me **working**—on the job and around my crew. Clipboard clutching and briefcase carrying is suicide in this profession, it doesn't make sense even for management.

5 **Bad Weather:** Can't be blamed on anyone, not even God, but the results of bad weather, both outside and in, sure are a janitor's problem. Not only the tracking of mud and slush, but the extra clothes worn and left around, the damage, falls, snow plowing and traffic, and then of course the heat regulation in the building. Everyone is either too hot or too cold! My company contracted to clean a 3-million square foot building in Atlanta. Four thousand people worked in there and on a rainy day it was havoc. They came in the building between 8 and 9 o'clock, dripping, crowding, slipping, and dropping things in big puddles of water while taking off their coats. And whose fault is any water on the floor? The **janitor's**, of course.

Your Cleaners May Need an Attitude Adjustment, Too

Our cleaners, egged on by the seemingly endless stream of client complaints, often develop an entirely negative attitude of their own toward "those miserable messers" they "have to clean up after." How can you help your cleaners have a better attitude towards the clients and building occupants they clean up after?

Tell them my favorite story:

When my company contracted to clean the famous Sun Valley resort complex, one of our duties was to set up conventions. During a big reception, one of my supervisors, Harry, in his college letterman's jacket and me in my church suit were hanging close to the entryway, policing up dropped glasses, etc., from the cocktail party in progress. A slightly tipsy and overweight reveler stumbled, spilling his drink and tray of chicken liver all over the carpet. He pointed to the mess and barked at the two of us, "Clean that up, boy!" I whipped a monogrammed silk hanky out of my back pocket, fell to my knees, and started sopping it up. Harry was appalled... "Why, I wouldn't do that for that big slob in a million years!"

"Listen, Harry," I told him, "whether that guy is a slob or not and whether he's right or wrong is irrelevant. We are professional cleaners, paid to clean, regardless of the circumstances, just as a doctor is bound to save the victim's life, regardless of what his character or reputation or even his actions may be. It's a matter of pride—we can't control others but we can control ourselves. It isn't the dirtiness of the duty; it's simply the duty. If it weren't for the slobs, you and I wouldn't be working here."

Or as one janitor said smilingly to someone about a nasty mess left for him to clean, "It may be crap to you folks, but it's my bread and butter."

Teach your cleaners that clients don't "cause us to work"—that **is** our work. It's our entire justification for existence as a profession.

Another tack you can take with them is **ahead vs behind:** this is admittedly psychology, but convincing people they're cleaning up to get tenants prepared or ready for work or a special event motivates them ten times more than the feeling they're cleaning up behind or after people.

The better you treat and work for your clients, the better their attitude will be toward you, and the less "abuse" cleaning and repair work you will end up doing.

The custodians were constantly complaining about people spilling and leaving popcorn all over the place. One night, we threw a training session and served lots of popcorn which the custodians ate plenty of—and spilled even more. We dismissed the session and everyone walked out. "Whoa," the leader hollered, "aren't you people forgetting something?" "What?" they asked.

"The popcorn you spilled."

Their reply: "Oh, the custodians will get it."

—Dwayne Gray

Break Time Image

This may sound like a reversal of good public relations and of the direction I have recommended for getting known and appreciated. However, as a cleaner, I would **never** take my break out in public. The public wants to see us working. While on duty we're the servants of the building. When you've seen a waitress off duty, on a break, sitting at a table with the guests, smoking a cigarette and visiting, have you ever had the feeling, "Hey, why don't you wait on me?" Or "So now I'm invisible—can't you see I need some more coffee?" It hurts her image. Likewise, whenever the cook comes out of the back and sits down at a table with the customers it really looks bad and detracts from his professionalism. We should recognize these normal feelings and avoid the situations that create the same kind of impression.

Our dress and the spirit of our work doesn't allow us to casually mix in with the public while we work. The average John Q. Public thinks that janitors are lazy and overpaid and just hang around. They seldom see us working corridors during the dark hours; they only see us during two or three coffee breaks per day. How will that mold and fix the public's opinion of us?

So first, have off-duty personnel wear jackets or other clothing over their uniforms if they need to be moving through the building during off time. If a tenant needs a janitor— say a spill has occurred—and they see a uniformed employee walking down the hall, the tenant doesn't care if the janitor's on a break or hasn't started the shift yet. He wants help now and he'll only be irritated if the janitor says, "Call maintenance and get a janitor on duty." Covering the uniform will help somewhat, but also train your people that they're janitors 24 hours a day (see Janitorize Your Life, Chapter 8).

Second, have a place your staff can safely and candidly take breaks—away from public view and interruption.

Cleaning P.R. Overkill

Being liked and personable as a custodian is a good thing, but like everything else it can be overdone. We sometimes are like friendly dogs, crushed when we get no attention.

Then when someone finally does show us some affection we leap on them, lick their hands and face, even slobber on them. He's a good dog until he jumps on you, barks or bites—then he's blown it... same with us.

A couple of guidelines here so you don't find yourself over the line:

Be friendly, but use your mouth to smile more than talk. Work for a two-word relationship. Any two words will do as you greet or pass. It won't slow down either of you or cause a traffic jam or safety hazard:

"Good morning."
"Great day."
"Clean, huh?"
"How're things?"
(Or invent your own expressions.)

Another good way to get friendly but not cozy is when asked a question like: "What kind of cleaner is that you're using?" Give a quick answer, but offer to drop off some information later. They'll love you.

Overkill in this area slips up on us so gradually that most custodians don't realize they're spending 2 or 3 hours a shift just talking! And it doesn't help the person who's working after hours to avoid the chitchat of other office workers, who wants to catch up on badly needed, deadline projects.

The over-friendly cleaner is so anxious to serve and show goodwill that they start getting the mail for the office, then they carry stuff, then they jump-start cars, even drive the car—pretty soon they're fixing the car—and all the while cobwebs are creeping into the janitor closet. I've met cleaners you can't get away from—they smother you. I quit dirtying up the place just so they wouldn't show up!

Does Our Work Really Matter?

As I mentioned early in this book, one of the reasons cleaning people have a need to be motivated continually is because the results of their work are instantly destroyed. While the work of other professionals—woodworkers, engineers, ballplayers, artists, teachers, etc., is recorded, published, admired, cherished and preserved, ours lasts 24 hours (usually less), and then we have to do it over again… and again. This routine, of course, encourages the habit of taking us for granted, because even if the public, our company, or our bosses really appreciate what we do, they can't thank or praise us or take official notice of every 24 hours of cleaning, so they seldom do it at all.

So the question you always need to answer for your employees is:

"DOES OUR WORK REALLY MATTER?"

What can you do or say by way of an answer? A gold watch or plaque thanks the person for endurance and service, but it doesn't really say that his service matters. People will work long hours—even free—when they know their work matters

This is a letter of resignation. Does one resign from being a janitor?! I don't know. I will continue working through the end of April. I just don't have the enthusiasm that, hopefully, someone else out there ~~does~~ has in cleaning offices. It's too much like work. Sounds funny, it's true. I need to ~~s~~ have a job where I deal more w/ people. Also, sorry, it's not working out

Sincerely,

P.S. —We need T.P.

to someone. How do you make cleaning matter?

• Continually point out, both seriously and humorously, what things would be like if we didn't show up (if there were no cleaners).

• Make it clear that ours isn't the only occupation that has to manage, and continue, to do a good job in spite of an aura of "impermanence." A cook's work gets treated even more brutally from beginning to end than ours!

• Other people's jobs may produce important products like watches, bread, and bicycles, but ours is alive and active, and giving every minute.

• Make them realize that the physical end result of their job may not last but the feelings our work creates do last and change the quality of lives. That's more important than adding a few more products to the world any day!

6 Motivation
in the Heart of the Job

Upgrading and motivating your cleaning crew starts **before** you hire them. There's no surer path to enthusiastic performance than starting with the best you can get.

Hiring

If the interviewer believes that anyone can be a janitor, you've got the wrong person doing the hiring. Careless hiring practices are self-destructive. One loser in a group of five willing, loyal maintenance people can cost you all five.

Don't take the leftovers or let people dump failures out of other departments into the cleaning staff. A high percentage of those beating a path to your door for a cleaning job (sad to say) are those who can't get a job anywhere else or can't hold a job. They seem to think that regardless of their lack of skill or their poor employment record, they can always be hired as a janitor. If the employee feels this way at the start, you're multiplying your motivation and image problems by hiring them. You can't expect to be choosing from a corps of Mr. and Mrs. Americas, but you can find some outstanding people. One positive, motivated leader on a staff of twenty will work wonders.

There are good qualified people looking for maintenance jobs, especially part-time jobs. One hour of careful interviewing and then properly orienting a new maintenance person could save you 20 hours of replacement time. One or two poorly chosen employees can cause more turnover and turmoil than all other reasons combined.

Point Out the Positives When You Hire

By the time most of the cleaners of the world get hired, they are quietly mouthing the famous line, "It's a dirty job—but somebody's got to do it." You might as well send a kid out to play in the haystack with a box of matches. Make it clear to every one of your new and on-board people that this is a full-scale and first-class profession.

Go Over the Benefits of the Job Point by Point...

Good Hours: While "janitor hours" may be less desirable for some, many appreciate the quiet and the opportunity of working without constant surveillance. Part-time janitors assigned specific hours can usually modify their schedule in case of emergency or by prior arrangement as long as the work is completed before the opening of regular business hours.

There aren't many jobs with this kind of flexibility.

No Hassle: As you watch dozens of ill-mannered people crowding around a food or retail stand, yelling, complaining at waitresses or clerks for eight hours straight, you can appreciate a janitor's job—alone in a building or with only a few other cleaners.

Almost every job involves some pressure, but this is not so with janitor jobs. A janitor works unhassled, where it is relatively quiet. In fact you can almost rest emotionally.

Safety and Security: Working inside a locked, warm, well-lighted building, many times with piped in music, is indeed a good situation.

Plenty of Exercise: Automation and convenience are leaving people overweight and physically soft. Janitor work has plenty of walking, light lifting, bending, stair climbing, etc., to keep you in great shape, if you hustle at your work. Janitor jobs are physical and jobs like them are getting harder to find.

Pay: By contracting, or doing extra work, a janitor can make better money than most people realize.

Education: The opportunity you get in a cleaning job to learn not only valuable skills, but about places and people, can't be matched—you see and hear everything. This is a multi-faceted job that develops hidden talents. The experience and broad-based development possible here will only add to your personal and professional worth. Right on the job you are able to observe all kinds of business operations and procedures that will give you a wealth of experience and information. You'll find most maintenance people are better informed than the average worker.

Social Interaction: A full or part time job here gives a person a chance to meet new and interesting people at their choosing and to form rewarding relationships which are renewed continually.

Being Needed: People *need* you. When cleaning is missed, you are missed—you count here! Plus, talk about a job to save the environment and help mankind. Name me any thing with more merit than cleaning. Whether cleaning up society or the world, our best champion is the cleaner.

Personal Growth: Contrary to most people's view of janitor service as "menial work," it requires good observation, good organization, and an abundance of responsibility.

Home Sweet (and Clean) Home: Professional cleaning skills, shortcuts, tools, and techniques will carry over into your personal life at home. You'll live a cleaner, happier existence and cut the time (and money) you spend on maintenance in half, giving you free time to spend with family and friends, and do the things you really like to do. (You'll be popular with the neighbors, too!)

Training Can Be a Great Source of Motivation and Image Building

Training in the maintenance field is more than teaching cleaning skills, such as mopping and window washing. These can be learned with minimum formal instruction, and then the finer points of the art of janitoring will be developed on-the-job under the direction of a good supervisor.

If I had only ten hours to train someone to become an efficient and productive janitor, I'd spend eight of the ten hours on attitude development. Here's a job that has a built-in stigma: the janitor, low man on the totem pole. Forget the technicalities of the job for a minute and let your people know that they're important to the company, that their contribution is as important as that of any of the employees. Let them know what you expect from them by way of appearance, punctuality, etc. Let them know that there is someone they can go to with their concerns and clearly identify this individual. Above all, let them know that you recognize them as an important part of the function of the company.

The last two hours of training you can then spend teaching the basic skills required on the job and in orienting the new person to his own area of responsibility.

Where is one good place they can go to learn those basic skills (as well as all the ingredients of a winning attitude)? After fifteen years of writing books about housecleaning, dejunking, how to be a better employee, painting, and how to run a cleaning business (30+ titles so far and more on the way)—I finally penned the most-asked-for topic: training for the front-line cleaner. It's called *The Professional Cleaner's Personal Handbook*.

I started with "The Varsity Manual," the training manual my company uses to train our 2000+ cleaners, then I added and expanded it.

Conduct Training & Upgrading Meetings

Like coaches, leaders have to rally their people around them. Training sessions in powerful settings can win and weld comradeship. If done well these will be a fun and inspiring experience, like a coach's pep talk, the President's State of the Union address, or an officer's call to charge. Use training sessions to spearhead improved production and spirit. Here are some ways to enrich get-togethers like these:

- Keep meetings short, packed, and to the point
- Hold them often
- Always be fully prepared
- They can be a surprise, for example, to introduce a guest or visitor
- Let crews speak and participate
- Don't allow negativism (moaning and groaning)
- Start and end promptly
- Use props and visuals—pass around, let everyone hold and feel them
- Have some exhibits
- Spice things up! Hold the sessions in different places
- Be sure to invite outsiders such as administration, interested students, and others.

Introductions

I've found a great way to communicate with and build people (and it works for both management and frontline cleaners). Whenever I introduce a speaker I give the person's name and a quick summary of their best virtues. Then I turn things back to them, for example: "This is Tobi Flynn, she is the one who has personally designed, laid out, and marketed all these books you see around you. Who are our best customers, Tobi?" Or, "This is Kathy Alley, the boss of the entire mailorder operation and the only person to beat me to work every morning—even when I come in at 5:30. Do you ever get any sleep, Kathy? " Or, "This is Walt Carte, the one who keeps the lobby floors looking like a sheet of glass—and for how long now Walt?" "22 years!"

Sample Agenda

Opening and greeting	You (Welcome and make introductions)
Report good news	You or assigned person (read any praise letters, note awards, promotions, work anniversaries, etc.)
Humorous Janitor Story	Take turns among crew (everyone has at least one); try to limit these to 3-5 minutes each
Challenge (game/project)	Anything from "Smell and Tell" to a crossword puzzle, that gets everyone tuned in to the subject
Business/program	Speaker (see above for how to introduce them) Show a video, demo a new system or machine Take a trip or tour Plan a special event, parade or assembly Elect a representative for convention (or any of 100 other exciting happenings)
Question/answer session	Let everyone talk—make it their meeting!
Refreshments	(Including punch served in a toilet punchbowl)
Distribute material	Always have something tangible for them to take away with them—a handout, flyer, or prize.

Seminars and Training Sessions

The occasional classroom-type get-together with a speaker or "sales pitch" of some sort is generally more valuable from a morale standpoint than for the actual information received. A get-together like this says: "You are worth the time and money to do this." Be sure to choose good speakers and remember, the size of the fee you pay them isn't always the main issue. I was with a group once that paid a famous newsman $9,000 for the presentation he delivered and it wasn't nearly as good as a couple of people in their own ranks could have done. The message from the speaker isn't always the valuable one—the fact that you have arranged the seminar says: "You are important." And being important is motivational and image building.

Let your people actively participate in the training, too. Nothing increases performance like having the opportunity to teach others.

The only way people become great is by being exposed to great things.

The best way to build a first-class organization is to involve first-class people. A sharp person from another company or another operation, a good contractor, or well known professional mixing in and working on the job with the crew for a week or two is an excellent way to teach new skills and inject new ideas.

Provide Adequate Job Specs, Documentation, and Direction

People feel a lot better when they know exactly what is expected of them. Nothing is worse for morale than confusion. Blame-throwing and arguments always result. Yet it's a common practice to turn the crew loose under the direction of a supervisor who isn't sure of scheduling and cleaning frequencies and other requirements of the building. Things are missed; things are duplicated; things are only half done. Many special areas like computer rooms and high security areas have only oral directives and no one knows for sure what is required to meet specs. Specs and documentation don't have to be elaborate, in fact, the simpler the better. But they should make absolutely clear what is to be done, how to do it, when you do it, and how much time it should take.

Expect a Lot

Make sure everyone on your staff is carrying a full workload and is producing to the maximum. People may moan and groan over a heavy workload, but they actually **thrive** on it.

People love to do better and go beyond the average of what is expected of them.

Nothing motivates like knowing we can do a tough job well. Likewise, nothing breeds boredom like a job that is unchallenging. This makes a person drag out a 4-hour job into 8 hours just to complete the shift.

A person handling a full load covers more ground and has more adventure. They'll also have less time to sit around and think how depressed they are.

I've found that in many cleaning operations, staff members can be asked to produce up to 30% more without any complaints. In fact a little more responsibility often gets them **more excited and enthusiastic**, provided it is a **fair workload**.

Try challenging your staff members more. You'll be surprised at the results.

Make Regular Inspections

You should be doing this anyway, for good quality control. If done right, inspections not only help assure the cleanliness level of a facility, they motivate people. Inspections say, "We care enough about what you do to look at it."

This is especially important in a field where the work is as "perishable" as it is in cleaning. Inspections are an official chance to notice and appreciate those shining floors and sinks and mirrors before they're dirtied back into invisibility. Regular inspections, conducted in a

positive manner, will be appreciated and an image builder.

Eliminate the gripe and chew session while you're at it. Somewhere along the line, someone thought that these sessions of assembling the employees and really "giving it to them" was an effective way of shaping them up. It generally alienates them. People respond better to positive recognition than they ever will to fear of job loss. This is the inspection form my company uses:

Quality Control Inspection Form

For General Building Cleaning
To be used monthly for each building contract.

Building _____ Floor/Area _____

Address _____ Supervisor City _____

Today's Date _____ Inspector _____

POOR | FAIR | GOOD | EXCEL.

1. ENTRANCE — Mats, Carpet; Glass, Metal Surfaces; Corners; Floor
2. LOBBIES — Dusting; Floor Appearance; Sweeping, Vacuuming; Spot Cleaning; Fixtures; Water Fountains
3. ELEVATORS — Treads; Lights; Walls, Doors; Floor, Carpet
4. CORRIDORS — Sweeping, Vacuuming; Floor Appearance; Baseboards; Spot Cleaning; Water Fountains
5. STAIRWELLS — Rails, Walls; Steps, Landings
6. RESTROOMS — Dispensers, Hardware; Sinks; Floors; Mirrors; Partitions; Toilets, Urinals; Waste Cans; Walls, Doors
7. OFFICE-EQUIPMENT AREAS — Carpet Spotting; Furniture, Equipment; Door Kick Plates; Phones, Lamps; Walls, Doors, Spot Cleaning; Glass, Metal Surfaces; Corners; Floor
8. RESILIENT TILE FLOOR — Corners & Edges; Appearance (Shine & Gloss); Sweeping and Mopping
9. WINDOWS — Glass; Frames; Blinds
10. CAFETERIA — Tables & Chairs; Walls, Doors, Spot Cleaning; Trash Containers; Dusting; Floor Appearance; Baseboards; Corners
11. JANITOR CLOSETS — Cleanliness, Organization; Supplies; Equipment; Required Manuals & Forms
12. MISCELLANEOUS — Policing Outside; Sidewalks; Phone Booths; Other _____

	POOR	BELOW STANDARD	GOOD	EXC	QUALITY POINTS
1. ENTRANCE	3.5	5	6.5	8	
2. LOBBIES	3.5	5	6.5	8	
3. ELEVATORS	1	2	3	4	
4. CORRIDORS	1	2	3	4	
5. STAIRWELLS	1	2	3	4	
6. RESTROOMS	6	9	12	16	
7. OFFICE-EQUIP AREAS	12	18	24	30	
8. RESILIENT TILE FLOOR	3.5	5	6.5	8	
9. WINDOWS	1	2	3	4	
10. CAFETERIA/LOUNGE	3	4	5	6	
11. JANITOR CLOSETS	1	2	3	4	
12. MISCELLANEOUS	1	2	3	4	
	37.5	58	78.5	100	

TOTAL QUALITY POINTS →

COMMENTS:

_____

_____

_____

Does this customer have any additional service needs?　　YES ☐　　NO ☐

You Can Motivate and Make a Difference

For the three most often forgotten little things that motivate our cleaning folks, I would suggest:

1. Pay on time. Many of our cleaning people are working two jobs and plan to the hour when they will get their checks to cover something, buy something, or go somewhere. When checks are even fifteen minutes late, it is often devastating. Cleaners often don't have a cash cushion, so late paychecks are super destructive to morale and loyalty.

2. Include all the family. Even though only a single person may be actually working for you, the rest of the family is involved in his pay. And they can be one of the best turnover reducing factors going. For a few extra dollars, if the "family" is included in dinners, trips, and incentives that family will suddenly be a solid support for your business. They may even end up working for you or finding others to work for you. Loving your people, and their kids and parents is a great way to get people to love and treat your business better.

3. Surprise tips and trips. A surprise ticket to a ballgame, to see parents, go to a special performance of some kind, ski lift tickets—anything you know they would like but "can't" (or won't) afford. Spend the $20 or $50 or $100, or even a little more at a surprising and unexpected time and you will get a 100% return on your money. It won't be the $20 that did it, but the signal that "you care" and are aware they exist.

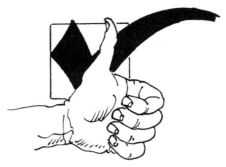

Personal Touch Checklist
(Small ways to tell your cleaning people they're important and that you and others care!)

- ☐ 1. Hand them their paychecks (when you can) instead of leaving them in a box or mailing them.
- ☐ 2. Give some small cleaning souvenir (even a putty knife) for birthdays.
- ☐ 3. Give them birthdays off with pay. Find out when their birthdays are, don't ask them.
- ☐ 4. Share or give those discount tickets or coupons that company heads always get.
- ☐ 5. Clean or help clean up their area on occasion.
- ☐ 6. Have them teach you how they do their very best skill (you both will benefit).
- ☐ 7. Bring in pizza before or after work for a 20-minute meeting/feast—always works!
- ☐ 8. Enlarge a letter of praise from a client or tenant and post it on the bulletin board, write in your comments, too.
- ☐ 9. Once in a while treat them to a steak at the local family steakhouse, (inexpensive is okay).
- ☐ 10. Make a personal phone call expressing pleasure right after a good job (not a month later).

50+ Ways to Say "Good Job!"

I'm proud of the way you worked today.
You're doing a good job.
Nice job!
Hey, you've really got it down.
Boy, you really know how to go after it.
That's the best you've ever done.
That's the best it's ever looked!
That's it!
Congratulations!
I knew you could do it.
That's quite an improvement.
You sure have figured it out!
Now you have it.
Good show!
You're learning fast.
Keep working on it, you're getting better all the time.
Good going.
Who would have thought it was possible!
You've really topped yourself this time.
I don't think I've ever seen a better job.
I hardly recognize this place.
It looks like a new _____.
It's never looked this good.
You've gone beyond my wildest expectations.
This _____ really sparkles/shines.
You sure know how to go the extra mile.
Wow, this gets an A+.
What a transformation!
I know where to go when I need something done right.
I really like your style.
Man, when you tackle something, you do it right.
I think this is great.
You should feel really good about this.
How in the world did you manage to do it?
I guess you know this is a great improvement. I hope you feel good about it.
How'd you get it so clean?
It's a real pleasure to see such a good effort.
I always look forward to using the restroom after you've cleaned.
My, I can see myself in that sink!
It's just amazing what you can do with a bowl swab!
Your mama would be proud.
Beyond belief!
Incredible!
Amazing!
Beautiful!
Bravo!
Not bad!
Great!
Terrific!
I'd like to take credit for that myself.
You just amaze me.
I feel like you read my mind.
If I only had another employee like you, I could retire.
When I really need someone to count on, I look for you.
I'm really proud to have you on our team.
When I need inspiration, I just look at the job you've done.
I'm speechless!
You really work wonders.
You're indispensable to me.
I had to do a double take because I couldn't believe what a good job you'd done.
You've truly accomplished some amazing feats.
You're so good, you make the rest of us look like we're going in reverse.

There Are Two Sides to Everything, Including Cleaning:

Brain dead to job

Eyes to look for a way out of work

Ears to hear all the negatives

Words that complain

Shirking shoulders

A heart yearning for something else

"Breaktime" stomach

Elbow to lean on

Clock to watch

Butt to drag

Just looking for a handout

Resting knees

Lagging legs

Feet just to stand on

Sole to tread water

Brain to figure out a better way

Eyes to see what needs done

Ears open for opportunity

Words that promote cleanliness

Sharing shoulders

A heart in the job

"I can take it" stomach

Elbow grease to get the job done

Clock to race to do more, better

Buns that hustle

Helping hands

Knees willing to bend to get the corners

Leaping legs

Feet to speed towards the job

Whole "soul" in profession

Help your cleaners pick the right side and stick to it!

7 Motivating

in the Meat and Potato Issues

Money

If you're looking for money, you can clean **out** the bank (rob it) or clean it up (be a janitor). Cleaning it up is a slower way to get it than cleaning it out, but the future is sure better. That about summarizes the cleaning profession's relationship to money. Very few have gotten filthy rich in it, and those who have made some big bucks have been in it for a long, long time, and have put in long, long hours.

Remind yourself and your cleaners, too, that people don't get rich as ministers, butchers, bakers, forest rangers, receptionists, and 400 other professions besides cleaning. The good money in cleaning is long range, and with a little patience a cleaner will see him or herself getting more than the

kitchen people, the delivery people, the secretaries, and a lot of other departments. Part time it'll take you even longer because this is generally catch as catch can and it takes a while to prove value. But being a large profession (9 million of us), there's a lot of room for promotion and upgrading (and that good money) within the trade and the industry, more so than in many.

Meanwhile, most all of our competitors are paying minimum wage for their production workers, so we have to be somewhere in there too, to be competitive. We'd all like to be able to pay our people top dollar, but the competitive bid process usually limits us to "market average" wage rates, and that's usually around minimum wage. We may not be able to do much about the low basic pay rate, but there are some things we can do to up the motivation quotient when it comes to money:

• Employees in the cleaning business accept the low wages because that's all they can find and they really need the money. If paychecks are even one day late I've seen employees fall completely apart. Never forget that payday is the big reason most of these people are working. They live for that check. Just because you can wait for **your** money if business is down or accounts are slow, they can't. Whatever you do, be on time and exact and accurate with their money.

• Even within the restrictions of the cleaning business economy you can pay more if your people are more efficient. It's important to communicate this because your people will be anxious to know how they can advance and get raises.

RAISES

So when can and should you offer raises? In cleaning this is a little tricky because "clean" is hard to measure. Working hard and doing a good job are pretty abstract terms—how do you define how hard is hard and how clean is clean?

You'll have to set a quality level (based on inspection) and a production level (based on how much has to be done in how much time). If your employees can accomplish both of these, they deserve a raise, and future raises as they increase quality and production.

All of us are over-optimistic about our ability and application. When I used to interview and hire a person, I

would say, "We will start you at the regular $3.50 per hour." (They'd only expected to get $3.35.) "And if you're an outstanding producer, in time you can work up to $7.00 per hour." At the end of the first month when I'd call them in to terminate them for total non-production they'd honestly think they were being called in for that $7.00 raise, and really expect it on their final check.

Make sure your agreements are clear. If you promise a raise or a bonus, then write out exactly when and make it 100% clear; don't say, "if you do well, you'll get a raise" because everyone thinks they "do well." Say instead: "If you can get your production up to 3,200 feet per hour, and can hold a quality index of 85 or better, you will get a raise of 50 cents per hour." Then you've eliminated all wild thoughts and smoldering resentments, and you also won't be stuck making a value judgment in a squirmy situation. They'll know at the end of the time whether they have it coming or not. And they'll realize that they, not you, determined whether or not they deserved it.

Benefits

Benefits are something that **should** motivate our employees, but they're rarely appreciated. Often employees aren't fully aware of them. Too many people think sick leave, hospitalization, profit sharing, pensions, and social security contributions just come with the territory. They don't realize that someone is paying thousands of dollars a year for these things. So it's up to you to sell them on the benefits you give them. Write them down, put them in a visual form and show them to your employees, and mention them at every meeting. It says, "Yes, we appreciate you and have a place for you—just look at what we're actually paying you above and beyond your salary."

It means a lot to employees when they realize all you're putting into employing them. I've seen employ-

ees overwhelmed, or filled with new appreciation for the company when they find out the company is matching their Social Security deduction, or how much the company pays for Worker's Compensation and health insurance, or that they offer a scholarship plan for employees' children.

Promotion and Advancement

Most people will put a lot more energy and interest into something if "it's headed somewhere," if it has the potential to become something more than just the hours they put into it today. Just knowing there's opportunity for advancement is an inspiration to many workers. What can you tell your cleaners about the possibilities for promotion within the cleaning field?

When my cleaning business was in its very early days of development and growth, an exciting thing happened. I did contract work then for four executives who were quite high up in the management of the Bell System, four of the biggest wahoos of what was then the world's largest company. In a meeting to sign some new contracts, one of them happened to mention that they all started their careers with Bell as janitors! Not that it was the lowest or the worst job imaginable, but it was, as it usually is, the most available position, the position open when they started.

Mainte-

53

nance work is the starting ground for millions of careers, and janitor work is no exception. A janitor position can be a good foot-in-the-door and stepping stone to the top. If moving up is the intention of your cleaners, then you should point out that they could hardly be in a better place to start.

• In no job will they learn more about what's actually going on in the company: about how it really operates and what makes it tick. In the maintenance department you have access to the whole plant or place, to people in every department.

• Nowhere could they learn more about the habits, personalities, strengths, and weaknesses of the customers and clients.

• No place will they have less competition.

• No place are there more varied and unexplored regions and areas to look good in, extra and beyond-the-average things to do to catch the higher-ups' eye.

• Nowhere will they have more influence on more of the daily functions of the company. In cleaning they affect or are involved in **budgeting, security, sanitation, safety, energy and utility use,** and **public relations**; they'll learn a lot about **organization, scheduling, personnel management, quality control, training,** and a lot of other essentials no one else knows how to, or wants to deal with.

In your meetings, speeches and interviews, be sure to point out that upgrading in life and work has lots of options, and in the cleaning profession, starting or working as a janitor you can:

• Work your way up in seniority and responsibility as a cleaner or maid, executive housekeeper, janitor, super-

visor, lead person, property manager, building manager, salesperson, foreman, trainer, consultant, specialist... the list goes on and on!

• Work up and advance to supervisor.

• Work up and advance to the slot of maintenance department manager.

• Work up and advance to a management slot in any other department.

• Work your way into a transfer to a different department or division of the company in cleaning, maintenance, or other areas.

• Work and learn so you can go into your own business someday. This is in fact one of the best "free" educations you can get.

• Work your way up to being a consultant, trainer, or writer in the cleaning field.

A promotion system is a great motivator. If the move from janitor to president is possible, let your people know it's possible and let them know how it can be done. Show them where they are today and where they can be in a year or five years from now and put the requirements to get there in writing. Then give them the opportunity. When there's a place to go, the good people will find a way to get there. The poor ones will weed themselves out. Be specific when it comes to requirements, make it clear that it's all based on production and results, not on tenure.

Cleaners Worry About Job Security, Too

We're all concerned about where we'll be ten years from now. Janitors are like any other workers, they're thinking:

• What's going to happen when I get older?

• I wonder how the company is really doing. If they fail will I have any warning?

• I wonder if the boss is thinking of contracting out my job?

• Is my union really going to save my job, no matter what?

• We're the first to lose our storage space and parking space; we have last choice of lunch hours and break times, so if anything happens, we'll be the first to go.

It's important to point out to your cleaning people that they have one real guarantee of security. They've whipped the image stigma of doing cleaning work to live, while so many others, even in times of dire need and joblessness, have refused, avoided, or quit anything that resembles cleaning up. When things get tough again it might appear that all the sharp, highly paid people will come down a notch in the company and push all the cleaning people out the bottom... it has never happened, during any recession, depression, Wall Street drop, or real estate downswing. The cleaning field has stayed static; none of the other

professionals even on the brink of starvation or losing their home would come into the ranks. Even when a "bigwig" wants to clean they seldom make it—they can't "go back" and catch the spirit of the thing. Cleaning has a nice self-weaning and self-weeding-out process. That's why the investment of sticking to the job means you'll always have a job.

The holder of a cleaning or maintenance job, too, is learning not just one but a number of allied "service" skills. And all the smart money says that skill and service jobs are the jobs of the future. Most of us who can clean well can be working anytime, almost anywhere, without an endless number of competitors trying to take our jobs.

All of this, of course, is based on real productivity—if you are a cleaner who is stretching 3 hours of work into 8 hours of time, then you don't have much security. But everyone is looking for a worker and a producer, and that is the ultimate security!

Last, But Not Least: Perks

Most workers today have a keen eye out for perks, or those little extras it might be possible to earn above and beyond the regular paycheck. Perks, or

55

rewards, should always be based not merely on time or effort, but superior production—which means speed and quality of work and the satisfaction of the tenants of the building. How clean is clean is always going to be a judgement, not an absolute, but with the proper Quality Control Program you can make a fair assessment. There are many options here.

PERKS THAT WORK FOR CUSTODIANS

• Set a reasonable budget for supplies and split the unused portion with your employees at Christmas.

• The upright vacuum they're using costs about $350. Tell them that with a good record, after one year, the vacuum is theirs. You'll be way ahead on this one. They'll keep the vacuum immaculate. It'll have no down time and will do a better job on the facility. Most vacuums are gone after a year, have 15 days of down time and $30 worth of repairs. You'll be ahead in profit and employee morale.

• If you have an in-house department and your employees are worried about a service contractor taking their jobs, have the contractor make a bid. Don't tell the cleaners how much it was, but promise them whatever cost they save under the bid amount at the end of the year (or six months) you'll share with them in a bonus or other compensation. You're sure to see less wasted time and supplies. An added bonus is that the inefficient employee either shapes up or ships out.

• Set a quality index for the building and have an outsider (contractor or other knowledgeable person) be the inspector and when the crew maintains or reaches its goal, pass them a

few extra bucks, or give them a paid day off once in a while.

• Take your cleaners on a trip or send them on an overnight seminar from time to time like all the other professions do. You'll be amazed at the esprit de corps it engenders. Remember how much fun and productive your high school field trips were? People never outgrow the desire to see new places. Hold meetings or schedule work occasionally at a different location, exchange assignments, move your people around—it does wonders.

• If you're a maintenance contractor, get your lead people and supervisors on your sales staff. Offer some kind of paid time off on a sliding scale for solid sales leads. You establish the size of target accounts. Then make sure they don't go around saying "Our firm is having a sales contest." Instead teach them to say, "I'm a custodian for XYZ Janitor Company, and we clean buildings just like yours. I think with our training program we could take care of your building the way you'd like to see it done."

56

Being (Remaining) One of the Gang

The worst thing that can happen in the cleaning industry is to have owners, managers, and supervisors who think they're above and beyond the actual cleaning. What's one of the biggest questions I get after forty years in the cleaning business owning a large company...? People wrinkle up their noses and ask, "But Don, you don't still work on the job any more, do you?" We too often grow to think we're above the realm of cleaning when we get to be the bosses. Remember and practice this most precious, important fact of success and motivation. In every profession, company, organization, family, or even personal relationship—there's always a heart and center of all feelings and mechanics. The heart and center is where everything to do with the people or purpose of a venture dwells; all the joys, all the costs, all the problems— everything. All the effort here is also what makes it "work," and too often because it is hard and stressful we pull out of the heart of what's going on and try to run, guide, boss, or manipulate things as a kind of absentee owner, from afar. Once we withdraw from the front, the firing line, the heart of what's happening, we lose a certain sensitivity and acuity of appraisal of feelings and needs. Reading reports about it once a month or broad over-views of the crew and work will leave you handicapped as to how to help and guide and encourage them. Be in-volved and stay involved in the heart of things as much as you can. Be a part, take part, don't keep yourself apart as too many leaders do. Trying to boss and prop people up with a pen instead of a personal appearance is a far cry from showing up and showing you care. Remember that needs, problems, setbacks, successes, tri-umphs—every aspect of your busi-ness—passes through the heart of the crew. If you aren't there, you can't feel the pulse.

8 Janitorize Your Life!

(or: Living the Religion of "Clean")

To change our image in the eyes of the public first we have to be noticed. We want everyone to know that we exist as people, and that our work is indeed a profession. Recognition by itself is a motivating force. We can't *make* people like us, praise us or appreciate us, but we can make ourselves known so that others can develop a good opinion of us.

We're not likely to be noticed if we saunter while we sweep, move along at an easy pace, wear street clothes, show minimal interest or enthusiasm—you can be sure that's not outstanding. It's the uncommon, the surprising, the better-than-the-rest that prompts people to take a second look, ask you a question, or pay you a compliment. It's that second glance

that makes it worth getting to work on time and doing a great job. One sure-fire way to get second glances is to stylize yourself a little.

What if cowboys didn't wear hats? What if people wore suits and ties to the rodeo? How much fun would you have? Creating the spirit of an event and the aura of your profession is important because it sets you apart. The trappings of different occupations are expected: the fireman's hat and boots, the carpenter's tool belt, the mail carrier's bag. It identifies and sorts the populace into groups that we know about and can deal with. We're comfortable with the trappings; they represent expertise. Proudly displaying the paraphernalia of our profession reminds people of the important

We all know how to westernize, and janitorizing is even easier! I went to a cafe once with a western name and the girls waiting table had little western skirts, cowboy hats, and the menus in holsters. That gave the place character. At one fully westernized restaurant I saw a high-class New York lady, who had gotten up to go to the ladies' room, come back and lean down and whisper to her husband, "What am I, Dear, a steer or a heifer?" They even westernized the restroom signs!

HEIFERS

STEERS

functions we perform, and it tells the public that we're indeed alive and happy and enjoying our work.

We've got a built-in theme—the cowboys westernize, the movie stars glamorize, and the janitors? They janitorize, of course.

Long ago I decided that I was going to be a janitor. I said, "Mom, if I'm going to be a janitor, I'm going to be the best darn janitor this country's ever known." I'm not only a janitor at work, I'm a janitor at home, in church, in life. Learn to flavor all your activities, dress, and comments with your proud profession—to wear the spirit of cleaning on your sleeve (or anywhere else you can dream up). You might even call this living the religion of "clean."

You and your crew will come up with dozens of ideas for janitorizing your printed materials, your vehicles, offices, and even your meetings. It promotes your profession and advertises it as a little out of the ordinary.

Here are some things I do—and that I've seen others do—to successfully janitorize:

• The plant in your office—put it in a ceramic toilet planter.

• Decorate your office with a buffer brush wall clock (see page 72) or outhouse bookends.

• Every business has a suggestion box. Just any old box'll do, but janitorize it and it'll look like this.

• Wear a squeegee lapel pin, and I even have a Janus wristwatch. You'll also see me sporting my specially-made squeegee holster (except through airport security!).

• Carry keys on a Toilet Plunger Key Chain or little Toilet Key Chain. I tell people it's the symbol of the royal order of plungerhood. It never fails to draw comment and give me the opportunity to preach the gospel of cleaning and the merits of my profession.

• I carry a Johnny Lip Light (there really is such a thing) with me everywhere I go. It's a little tool you use to inspect under the rim of a toilet and see if it's clean or not. Boy, does that get attention—and comments and worried looks. It's a reminder that we janitors care about doing a good job.

• Your briefcase—make it a genuine Toilet Attaché. I had an elegantly designed and detailed outhouse tooled in leather and made into a cover for the notepad I carry with me everywhere and use constantly. It serves my serious recording purposes—but it also gets a lot of amazed and admiring glances.

• You can even make yourself a toilet suitcase (I promise it'll get special handling by all the airlines). My custom-made toilet suitcase (see page 17) attracts instant attention everywhere I go, across town, across the nation, or across the ocean.

• My office is decorated with all sorts of cleaning mementoes, and the mailbox that stands proudly outside the entrance to my ranch home is made from a retired floor buffer.

• I collect and post jokes, cartoons, and poems that have to do with cleaning.

• I collect (and write) cleaning music. Someday I'm even going to come up with my own "Cleaning Man" theme song or entrance music.

• When greeting or meeting people I ask them, "How did your house look when you left?" or "I just washed a toilet with that hand..." (as I shake theirs) rather than a dull "How are you?"

• You can't use the word "professional" too much when referring to your employment.

"In my profession we..."

"My professional advice for that floor would be..."

"Most of the people in our profession are..."

• Start your speech off with, "Greetings and Sanitations... what did you expect from a cleaner!"

• We in the cleaning profession are in a position to see, hear, feel, and smell everything, have more varied and unusual experiences than any group of people I can imagine. We are everywhere, around every type of people, at every conceivable hour. We have access (keys) to more places than the boss or the owners have. Sure much of our job may be routine, so is every job, but there is so much humor, adventure, excitement, and knowledge involved that we really are in a dynamite profession. We need to write these things down, capture them before we forget. Keep a "cleaning journal." If you do, you'll find yourself using the material in it for training, teaching, performances, and speaking, as well as personal enjoyment.

Cleaning has more up/good times and positive effects on life than negative ones. However, eighty percent of publicity about cleaning is negative. The reason is we don't capture and share the fun side of it!

• When people are exchanging stories—at the table, around the campfire, or even on an airplane—I tell my cleaning stories. They're hard to top, and we cleaners know plenty of them (keep them in good taste, of course, and make sure that the identity of any clients involved is kept strictly out of it).

Jot down key phrases from your best stories on the back of a business card and carry it in your wallet, so you won't forget any. You can add the most remarkable anecdotes you hear from your fellow cleaners to your own experiences.

> I tell cleaning stories everywhere I go, and if anyone gets smart-lipped about my profession, I inform them that I'm the one who dumps their trash and cleans out their wastebasket at night, so I know all about them and even a little more. I smile and they're suddenly quiet and wondering... it works every time!

• Countries, communities, and families have, over the years, developed a or "coat of arms"—an insignia, symbol, or logo to visually represent and identify them. On tour in Great Britain I was impressed with the colorful and crisp claims of greatness depicted cleverly in these emblems and so I made one of my own, a cleaning coat of arms.

At the top is a toilet seat (held aloft by a man and woman's

arms), framing a portrait of Janus, the figurehead (or heads) of custodians everywhere. At the center is a shield emblazoned with the logo of Varsity, my cleaning company, and on either side of it are cleaning tools: broom, mop, scrubbee doo, sponge mop, and duster. At the bottom, in the banner, is my motto. It depicts a noble and indispensable industry.

• I also made handsome janitorized stationery, which proudly displays my custodial coat of arms. You can design your own, or even send a letter or note written on a roll of toilet paper. This wipes out any doubt that you're a committed cleaner!

• I sign letters with a janitor nickname, like "Don Aslett, King of the Toilet Ring," or "The Dean of Clean." I have over two dozen such humorous titles to choose from, and the more I tell people about them, the more they outdo themselves in giving me new ones! I even start letters with lines like "Jumping germs!" I'm a cleaner and I show it!

• When something is spilled in a store, on the sidewalk, at a party, in a restaurant, or anyplace, I jump right in and clean it up before anyone else can even get there. Carry a clean-up kit with you at all times (after all, doctors carry their little black bags). Saying "I'm a janitor" right at the start makes people relax in an awkward situation where they probably don't know what to do. Everyone around will remember your good deed (especially the person you help) and janitors as a whole will move up a notch in their

CLEANLINESS IS FREEDOM

eyes. I don't do this just to make a good impression either, it really makes me feel good to use my professional skills at a time and place where they're really needed.

• Wherever I go, I carry toilet erasers to give out to kids, toilet keychains or earrings to give to new acquaintances.

Buying and giving children pint size (their size) brooms and dustpans for Christmas or other special occasions really goes over well. Children love to play and "practice" with grownup tools or trappings and what could be better than a little training and conditioning in the concept of cleaning up after themselves?

Almost daily I see new chances to janitorize, to move a little closer to instant recognition.

Janitorizing knows no limits. Pictured here is a janitor at his wedding. Someone asked him how he liked his job and he parted his tux Superman style to reveal the janitorial company emblems sewn carefully to his best white dress shirt.

Little Things Really Communicate

Why do we spend $1.50—up to $5—on a simple greeting card? We could just write a happy birthday note or getwell message on a piece of paper and mail it, but it's going the extra mile that shows you care.

Small touches have no better place than in a profession where people least expect it—the cleaning field. In the last few years I've added a little pizazz to my business cards, stationery, and notes—and guess what? I often get as many comments about the paper as I do about my message.

Cleaning related cartoons, calendars, cards, note pads, and other messages say, "We exist as a department in this school or this hospital." Printed material stays around longer and goes much further than speeches, skits, etc. Save artwork and clever printed pieces that you come across and adapt these ideas to your own message, photos, or drawings on your own stationery and make it part of your communications.

The thank-yous and notes we send often include drawings, poems, songs, cartoons, etc. They're well appreciated and remembered, and mentioned to our cleaners again and again. Put out the effort to make your communications come alive. Following is a sample of a page we left for the telephone operators after we stripped a floor all night in the Rock Springs, Wyoming, telephone building.

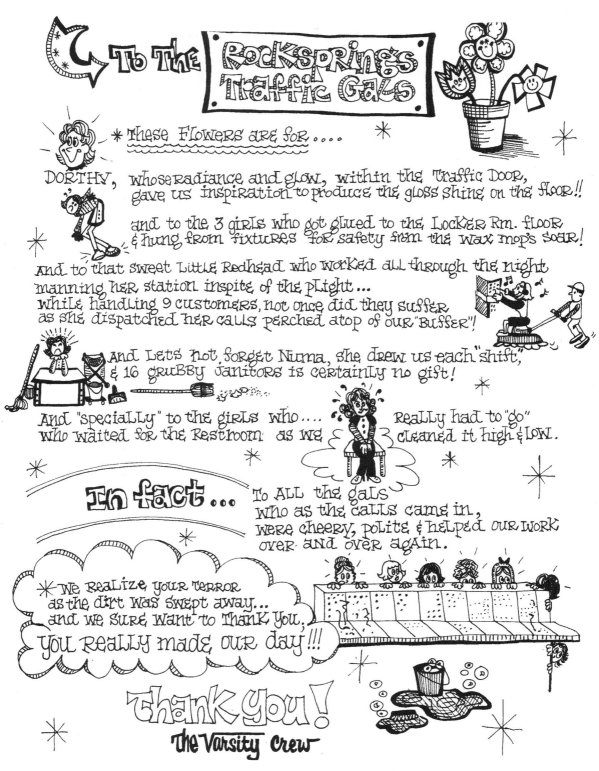

To The ROCKSPRINGS Traffic Gals

These Flowers are for....

DORTHY, whose radiance and glow, within the Traffic Door, gave us inspiration to produce the gloss shine on the floor.!!

and to the 3 girls who got glued to the Locker Rm. floor & hung from fixtures for safety from the wax mop's soar!

and to that sweet Little Redhead who worked all through the night manning her station inspite of the plight... while handling 9 customers, not once did they suffer as she dispatched her calls perched atop of our "Buffer"!

And Lets not forget Numa, she drew us each "shift", & 16 grubby janitors is certainly no gift!

And "specially" to the girls who.... really had to "go" who waited for the Restroom as we cleaned it high & low.

In fact... To all the gals who as the calls came in, were cheery, polite & helped our work over and over again.

We realize your terror as the dirt was swept away... and we sure want to Thank You, YOU REALLY MADE OUR day!!!

Thank you! The Varsity Crew

Janitorize the Menu!

Food can satisfy appetites and build bodies, but even better, if handled creatively, it can aid any cleaning event, by building images and refreshing attitudes. My first experience with janitorized food was when my wife baked a cake for a company dinner and decorated it like a building we'd just contracted to clean. Out of pipe cleaners she made little cleaning people on ladders, with buckets and brooms and placed them all over the "building." That sure personalized the cake to our profession—it even made the prime rib pale by comparison. Soon after, one of our managers used a factory-fresh toilet for a punch bowl at our next meeting (filled with lemonade, of course). From there on it's been fun to always try and

improve on the old punch and cookies theme.

There are no rules or bounds so you have a wide open field to come up with cleaning "refreshment" ideas. I'll share some of our successes to get you started. Remember, anything that draws attention to our profession in a positive way says something to the public. In this case your creativity will say it all and you won't have to say a word!

Cakes

Are one of the easiest things to janitorize. On my birthday, while I was teaching a cleaning Facility Care Course at

North Idaho College, the class baked a giant cake in the shape of a toilet, and wrote in blue frosting "Happy Birthday to the Toilet Man." The whole building got a piece of that "toilet" and was caught up in the spirit of cleaning.

The layers of a cake can match the floors of a building, or you can decorate it to represent one of your new contracts, or the building that a retiring employee has cleaned for years. Your local cake decorating supply store has candy, dyed marshmallows, specially shaped pans, and decorations that can help make a cake look like anything or anyplace you want.

Then there's the famous plunger cake—this will get 'em every time. You just make a round two-layer cake, with the top layer 1/3 smaller than the bottom, then use reddish-brown frosting to turn it into an authentic plunger base. Insert a dowel into the top for the handle, and it'll look like the real thing. Or you can convert this into a buffer cake by tilting the stick back to serve as the handle, and adding a couple of dough-nut or cookie wheels.

They'll polish it off!

Cupcakes can be shaped and decorated to look like mop buckets or other inhabitants of the janitor closet. Creative frosting or even a little plastic replica placed on top will look cute and say, "We have more fun!"

Cookies

Cookies are inexpensive and can easily be converted to all kinds of clever morsels. You can mold all kinds of cookie shapes by hand, or bend a strip of tin to make a custom cookie cutter. Or even cut cookies out individually to look like anything you want. You can use a cake decorator or a small paintbrush and plain old food coloring to help complete the effect. I've seen buffer brush cookies, chocolate chip keys, toilet cookies, even coconut dustmops. My friend Kathy from Spokane used oblong wafer cookies spread with a little frosting to make them sticky, then sprinkled shredded coconut on top. She stuck a large toothpick (you could also use a candy apple stick or small bamboo skewer) on for the handle and it became a delicious dustmop!

For our company meeting and training session one year, my wife made 4-inch sugar cookies shaped like the old outhouse on the farm, the early version of the toilets we clean. Once they were baked, she applied a little decorative frosting in a crescent moon and presto, a genuine rural retreat!

• **Buffer brush and pad cookies:** Any round cookie can be made to resemble some kind of a floor pad or buffing bonnet. These taste a lot better than an actual pad, and can even be used for a visual aid, to train while you eat!

Serve with Style

Not on silver trays, but something more practical. It goes without saying that you want a brand spanking new or freshly cleaned edition of any of the following for this purpose.

• Dustpans make the nicest serving trays. What other tray in the world has a handle you can really get a grip on? Great for appetizers, sandwiches, and cookies. Or even eat off them as plates and watch the reaction.

• A miniature ceramic toilet (often sold and used as a planter) is unquestionably the perfect cookie jar!

• Buckets can be used to serve all kinds of things, and we janitors have a big choice of "serving containers" here. You can even add a plastic bag "liner" to help keep the biscuits fresh and add authenticity.

• Serve bean dip in a baby potty chair, or in a ceramic toilet mug.

• A chocolate outhouse made from a simple plastic mold is a real attention-getter you can construct for only a couple of dollars—anyone can make them. Just melt some chocolate into the mold and put the pieces together when it hardens. I sell the mold in my catalog (see page 76). These are perfect for gifts or to sit in the middle of a brownie or fudge tray. Henry, a custodian in Coeur d'Alene, Idaho, when his turn for goodies came, made a clever rest stop (like the ones he cleaned in reality), with a chocolate outhouse and all the rest of the landscape.

Decorations with a Memorable (Maintenance!) Theme

Christmas, Halloween, Easter, Thanksgiving and all the other special days and events in the year are easily identified by decorations. Go to an insurance, food service, or auto industry convention and every decoration there is related to the spirit or subject of the convention. Yet at the hundreds of janitorial and cleaning supply sales events I've attended, seldom if ever do you see cleaning themes used as a backdrop or decoration. Cleaning decorations seem to have been relegated to the realm of invisibility, like we cleaners. I'm here to tell you—in fact show you—that cleaning-related decorations can help create respect and gain attention for our industry.

Take centerpieces, for example:

Who wants a flock of flamingos or frog pond fronds when you can have something much more appropriate to the occasion? Tiny cleaning motifs or tools tucked in with the flowers will make a professional bouquet that really dresses up the table and says "This is our profession! It's important to us, and we're proud of it." Some possibilities for the janitorial arranger: buckets or jugs as vases, spray nozzle "seed pods," johnny mop or lambs-wool duster "giant mums," Masslinn cloths folded and cut or tied into bright yellow blossoms. Rubber gloves inflated with helium and tied with ribbons sure beat plain old round balloons like everyone else has!

One way to make the centerpiece really attractive and help keep the trimmings from being "borrowed" is to wrap it in colored cellophane gathered at the top with ribbon like a gift basket.

When it comes to relaying messages to attendees, too, something cleaning-related handles the job just as well! Tie a clothespin to a handle of a small plunger and plant it on the table. Every person picking up a message will be smiling.

Think cleaning when it comes to holiday decorations, too. When we decorate a Christmas tree in the office, for example, we always sprinkle in mini toilets and TP garland.

Think! Whenever you need to decorate and find yourself starting to use the same old things used a hundred times before—what cleaning subject, supplies, or tools could be incorporated into the decorations instead? You'll never run out of ideas.

Don't Overlook the Motivational Power of Music

The "floosh-gloosh" rhythm of a toilet plunger at work isn't the only tune possible in cleaning. Music has played a big part in upgrading and motivating individuals, groups, teams and even armies and nations into commitment and dedication. Music lends spirit, and spirit is something often lacking in cleaning crews. Music breaks up routine and we have plenty of routine in our operations that could use some breaking up. This doesn't mean I think that passing out Walkman headsets complete with John Phillip Sousa tapes for cleaners to listen to is the answer. We don't allow our cleaners to listen to music while they're working—it slows production and causes accidents (the cleaner involved is always fiddling with, losing or hunting for the radio or batteries or extension cords or tapes). Then where should you use it? The same place everyone else uses it.

Think of it: when you attend a ballgame, pep rally, concert, movie, convention, or show—you see music used in every one of them. You don't, of course, want to use the plain old music the rest of them use, convert and alter it a little to fit.

Six years ago when I began my cleaning seminars, one group that introduced me didn't follow the old "And now let me introduce Don

Aslett" routine, instead they found the sheet music for the song "Mr. Sandman" and wrote some new words for it. When the curtain rose, instead of me, there were four women, all excellent singers and in perfect harmony they sang:

Mr. Aslett, teach me to clean
Bring down the cobwebs
Make my windows gleam
Teach me your tricks
So I'll enjoy it
But can I learn to like cleaning a dirty toilet!
Aslett, I'm in a mess
It's bound to ruin my happiness
So please come on and do your thing
Mr. Aslett, teach me to clean.
(They did all the "bum-bum" parts, too!)
Mr. Aslett, teach me to be
All clean and tidy, for my company
I need a maid, but they cost money
The kids just streak the walls with bread and honey!
Aslett, tell me it's true
There's really life after the housework is through
So please turn on your magic beam
Mr. Aslett, teach me to clean.

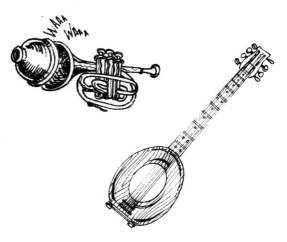

It went over so well with the audience that we suggested to other seminar sponsors that they use music to introduce the event and in the next several years dozens of different groups thought up clever musical introductions for my appearances. The music really made a difference. I even wrote a song called Betty Betterhouse, to the tune of "My Bonnie Lies Over the Ocean." I'd divide the audience into toilets, sponges, buckets, and other cleaning apparatus and then to that famous tune we sang:

Oh Betty went into the bathroom
To clean up her dirty toi-lets

At which time all the "toilets" would jump to their feet and, with a flushing arm movement, say "glug-glug!" And so on. It was a lot of fun, and the audience loved it.

A lot of popular songs (songs people know well enough to sing along with, or at least get your jokes!) of the past and present lend themselves to a clever turnaround, everything from "Mop Around the Clock" to "Sixteen Tons," from "My Bucket Runneth Over" to "The Hustle."

We all love music and have made it a part of every large company meeting or session, using live talent, tapes, instruments, or anything. In fact, one year at our annual meeting we staged a janitor musical and everyone participated, changing songs from "Take Me Out to the Ball Game" to "Take Me Out to the Floor Job." We even had a chorus line with mops and a janitor opera!

There are hundreds of ideas, songs, and talents right within your own ranks, all you need to know is that you can do it and that it'll do a lot to make your people feel their jobs are more than moping and mopping.

One group of cleaners imitated famous singers, altering their names to match, like Kidney Rogers, Elton John, Latrinee Lopez, José Flushiano.

One group converted a toilet seat into a banjo and guitar and called it a guitoilet. Another group did the limbo, only going under a pay toilet door!

Forming your own all-janitor band isn't a bad idea, either. Imagine your cleaners performing at the next holiday happening with some of these ideas taken from our janitor band (see page 101).

Don't be afraid to ask your staff for ideas—if you can't come up with any musically-related ideas, believe me, they can! Not a few cleaners are excellent or even professional-quality songwriters or performers. Bring their talent out, and let them help you bring your company gatherings to life!

You can let your imagination loose when creating instruments for a janitor band.

9 Awards

Make Motivation Easy, Don't They?

Most of us have been to Sea World or some other aquatic park where the seals and porpoises perform, and we love it. We enjoy seeing them do fantastic tricks, but did you ever think that it isn't the tricks that you like so much as seeing the performers get their rewards? After a gallant effort, the porpoise will rise up out of the water and hear the applause and cheers, and then wait for the promised delectable fish. Once the boss tosses a fish, the porpoise is unstoppable. He puts even more effort into the next jump and again, when the job is well done, he knows right where to go for the reward.

We all respond in about the same way. Like the porpoise, if we don't get appreciation and something tangible like a fish once in a while, we have a hard time staying excited about our performance. We've all received an award or reward sometime for going a little beyond the ordinary. We rise up out of the dust of our duties to listen for the applause and wait for our fish. Hardly a week passes now that I don't receive an award, gift or enthusiastic letter for my efforts as a speaker, writer, or show guest, and I can see that we just never get tired of being praised and appreciated.

Cleaning people don't have much direct contact with society. Lots of us do our work at night when no one is around. Our profession also isn't the #1 concern of our customers, and might never be. The bottom line is that we and our work are pretty inconspicuous and thus basically

69

unappreciated. We get few, if any fish. So finding opportunities to throw out a fish for fine cleaning work—coming up with some clever ways to show appreciation—will go a long way in upgrading and motivating your people. In the pages that follow I'd like to share some that really work, and I'm sure these will inspire you to think up others. Above all, we want to avoid the tired old things that "everyone gets all the time." These are simply so common and over-used that they have very little impact. Whenever you can, try to come up with custom tailored awards of your own—they're always the best.

The Old Standbys

• **Paper Certificates:** If you've never received any form of recognition, a certificate can have some meaning. But the ones given to janitors are generally an insult. They're mass produced on cheap paper and so poorly designed they often look unprofessional as well as unattractive. And the inscription is either impersonal or sloppily written. Rarely have I seen a certificate that's nicely done, with names hand inscribed in script. Certificates are like Xerox copies and plentiful these days. They aren't necessarily going to impress anyone, or cause a crowd to gather. If you use certificates or plaques, do them so well and so cleverly that they're something to be proud of and really worth hanging up.

• **Employee of the Month:** If done right and *consistently*, okay, but risky

and hard to carry out effectively. If you start a program like this and don't keep it up, it can end up a real negative.

The plaque hangs on the wall in July with "Employee of the Month" for January, February, March, but none since. The blank months bear silent testimony to the fact that the boss didn't really care enough to follow through. Do an Employee of the Month program well, or not at all. Half a job will backfire on you.

• **Lunch:** This can be a nice gesture, but don't expect an employee to do a backflip over a free lunch. We all get to dine out often enough these days that it's no big deal. The important thing to convey here is: "You are important to me. I want to spend some time with you and get to know you better. I enjoy your company." Make it dinner with their spouse once in a while and don't talk about cleaning, talk about them, and let them talk.

• **The Gold Watch:** Is another case where time and easy availability have eroded the old tradition. Thirty years ago, owning a fine watch was something impressive. Watches were handed down in families and had some real prestige and meaning. Today, a second grader can get a quartz watch with a calculator, two alarms and a video game for $9.95. Pen sets are in the same league.

Here are some events and accomplishments you may want to base awards and recognition on:

• **Outstanding Performance/Production:** Set tangible quality and quantity goals and make them tough enough that it's a real accomplishment to reach them. Have written records and clearly-communicated expectations so that awards like these will always be fair and unbiased.

• **Acts of Honesty:** These happen regularly, and most bosses miss the opportunity to capitalize on them (see p. 26). An employee finds money, a ring, a purse, whatever, and quietly turns it in so the owner can be found. Don't just give her a mention in the newsletter (most don't even get that). Even a $10 tip would be great. **This is an act of heroism, of honesty—a rare trait nowadays.** Get it in the local paper, and at the next company gathering have the janitor stand up and have the 700 engineers in the plant applaud. This accentuates the positive, induces more honesty from others, and strengthens the overall honesty level in your company.

• **Birthdays:** A common, but always appreciated way or excuse to recognize someone and show that you're aware of them. Everyone enjoys special attention on their birthday, a day (or shift) off with pay being the favorite.

• **Anniversaries:** Remembering an employment anniversary, recognizing tenure, sends a message home that the employee is important, needed and respected at work. Who doesn't need this vote of confidence?

One year, five years, ten years is a long time for a cleaner to stick it out. Awarding them something for this might mean another ten years with no turnover.

• **Suggestions, Inventions, or Other Contributions to the Company:** Employees constantly come up with ideas for better and smarter ways to do things, new sales approaches, maybe even new tools and machines. When these are put in action, everyone benefits. Sometimes we recognize the first one and feebly thank the originator. After that, million-dollar ideas are just "expected." Such contributions are an important occasion to give recognition and awards. You can also show appreciation and encourage people to further pursue their ideas with a meeting with the big boss, etc.

• **Transfers or Promotions:** Even a lateral move in a job is an occasion to say thanks for what the employee has done. Generally we wait for the big one, retirement. Just think of this a minute—that does little good for either the company or the employee. It's almost like never attending any of your friends' events or parties, then going to their funeral. Recognizing someone now, while they're still very much a part of your operation, will give them a better quality of life and give you much more results, and that combination just can't be beat. Recognition **now** will give them morale boosts when they need it most—while they're in the thick of the action. And it'll mean an improved attitude that can be translated into stronger performance, not just fleeting farewell feelings, however fond.

• **Illness or Injury:** Is generally a negative experience in a person's life, but it's one of the most positive opportunities for an employer to recognize and award an employee with affection, care, and help for home or family (see p. 29). In a situation like this, even an offer they don't accept scores a big "We love you and miss you at work" point.

• **Contests:** Are great if they're handled right. You can set up any kind you want: Best suggestions, greatest speed, smartest problem solving, least accidents, most compliments, least days missed, longest lasting vacuum, least complaints and endless others. Contests are stimulating and you'll usually get a lot of participation. Give a bike, a CD player, or some other useful item to the winner and leave it on display for three months before making the award. You'll get motivation and effort from all, no matter who wins.

• **Safety:** Your cleaning and maintenance people have more direct control over safety than anyone in the building. More so than the safety department. They work the late, dark hours with chemicals of all kinds, on slick floors, with electrical equipment, and other hazards. Accident-free time for them should be rewarded.

Customized Awards

Now that you have plenty of occasions and reasons for recognizing and rewarding, **what kind of quality awards can you give?** How can you do better than the old standbys?

Don't be afraid to design and make up some of your own awards. There are people in your organization full of ideas and talent. For example, mounting a miniature toilet plunger or squeegee tie pin (both available in my mail-order catalog) on a classy ribbon or plastic name plate would be simple and effective. What can you do? Well, let's customize a few things, starting with the gold watch:

• **Janus Watch:** Available from PortionPac Chemical Corp., this beautiful watch depicts two-faced Janus, the mythological god, able to see in both directions as guardian of the household and all treasures therein. PortionPac has other Janus custodial recognition items—write to them at 400 North Ashland Avenue, Chicago IL 60622-6382. (See also page 76.)

• **Buffer Brush Wall Clock:** It tells time, but it really relates to the job, and brings chuckles and comments ever after as it hangs on the wall. A real attention-getter that is easy and inexpensive to make. We all have lots of old buffer brushes around or just buy a new one. Lay out the person's name, nickname, or a clever title or expression on the surface, and carve it one-eighth-inch into the wood, using a common router. Then

72

sand lightly and paint in the letters, or stain and varnish them. Then for a few dollars you can buy a quality clock mechanism to mount in the middle.

• **The Formal Thank-You Letter:** I've received hundreds of awards and expressions of appreciation for community service, performances, etc., but one of my favorites resulted from an article I wrote about the telephone company. One day an exclusive looking envelope arrived in the mail. It was a personally written and signed letter of thanks and praise from none other than John DeButts, the Chairman of the Board of the biggest company in the world. Just a little page with a few words on it. But the fact that he took the time to write it and cared enough to send was more motivational than a $200 watch. Use company stationery, be sure to sign it yourself, and indicate on the bottom everyone who received a copy. A letter to an employee's spouse, or one of their children, or parents will have an impact you won't believe. Your letter will have lasting value, because it's tangible evidence they can show friends, hang on the wall, or put in a scrapbook.

• **Pictures:** Have you ever watched a person's reaction when they see themselves in a picture with everyone else? Our cleaning team is no different than the basketball team, 4-H club, or graduation class. Remember those old group pictures you keep and treasure? Why not provide professional, full-size photos of your custodial teams?

My company managers always have a camera with them. We take pictures of our people on the job, at play, or at lunch, and we display them or enlarge them and send them to the employees.

It only takes a little extra effort and expense to put a picture in a special frame, and once given it lives on forever and ever. It says, "We care—you are worth something!" Taking the time to frame a picture almost guarantees that it will be kept and displayed. (See also pages 30-31.)

• **Publicity:** Publicity is basically getting public attention. The more, the better, if the feat is praiseworthy. Publicity is the same as advertising, except publicity is free. Newspapers, radio and TV, in fact all the media search every day for fodder to feed the public, and will welcome any good human interest material you can give them. I've done thousands of media appearances in the last twenty-plus years and yes, this janitor has even had some top billings. Whenever you can get any of your people in the news, on the TV, or into the paper, do it! It'll often go farther than a fancy bonus. *Reader's Digest*, for example, runs a series on "Life In These United States." Now tell me, who has more experiences in life than cleaning people? They get a firsthand look at life that few others have.

Publication is one very good form of publicity you can use to build your people. One Christmas we published a book of janitor-contributed poems, short stories, and cartoons. The cost was minimal, and several years later still brings laughter and it tells the readers that our people are the most valuable asset we have. Remember all those funny stories, those incredible complaint notes, the jingles and the jokes from your business experiences? Collect them and share the message that maintenance work is alive, exciting, and fun.

• **Bonuses:** Money might be a satisfier, not a motivator as the experts say, but money talks to people! Any bonus is good, but a surprise bonus is the best! When an employee knows they have a bonus coming, it has less impact because they have most of it spent before they even get it. Its motivation value is minimized.

On the other hand, if you walk up to an employee on a Friday afternoon and say, "Things have really been going well around here, and you've had a lot to do with making it happen—here is a $30 bonus." They'll be ecstatic!

Lots of people count bonuses as part of "What they have coming anyway,"

and in fact become very judgmental about why and to whom one is given. Try a surprise once with your cleaning folks and observe the results.

• **Books and other Professional Materials:** This type of material is a good "time release" motivator. Most people are intensely interested in subjects closely related to their jobs and will appreciate the gift. And as they become more educated, they'll also be more dedicated. A personal subscription to a magazine or enrollment in a professional organization or course is a lasting gift. And videos or cassette tapes will be played over and over, saying, "thank you, thank you" each time.

• **Don Aslett Autographed Books:** When I speak at a convention, often the sponsor will give one of my autographed books to each attendee. The crew notices and likes it more than the trophy or plaque sitting on the table next to it. If you let me know ahead, I can autograph a book for any gift or occasion with the person's own name on it at no extra cost. (See order form at the back of this book.)

Here are just three of the more than thirty books by Don Aslett.

• You can even **Hold or Sponsor a Seminar for the Janitors and their Families:** What nicer award or gift is there than to put on a show for them, a real live presentation (not a canned broadcast) that involves them very directly, that they can personally experience and participate in.

The best kind are those which help your people develop themselves and feel more confident and valuable. Entertainment alone doesn't last very long. See Chapter 10 for many ideas.

• **Tickets to a Nice Restaurant:** I know the benefit of this seems to just get gulped away, but everyone, at least every once in a while, wants to go to a fancy restaurant and live it up—not with *you*, but with a companion of their choosing. A $50 restaurant certificate gets them a pretty nice meal.

• **Gift Certificates:** A $50-100 gift certificate to a local store—sporting goods, jewelry, clothing—is always a hit, often better than money because it takes away the guilt of spending money on themselves.

• **Trips and Travels:** The guide once stood up at the front of our tour bus in Hawaii and said, "You are the nicest, sharpest group I've had for a long time. What do you do for a living?" In unison we yelled, "We're Janitors!" The guide's face flinched in disbelief. Yes, cleaners like to go places too, but most don't because of money restrictions. Sponsoring a few of your people at cleaning clinics, field trips, a grand opening of another of your stores or branches, or even a pure pleasure destination like Disneyland is relatively cheap, and super motivational. Buy tickets, don't give money!

• **Novelty Gifts:** At a Chamber of Commerce speaking assignment once, I was presented with two gifts. The first was a beautiful bronze statuette—valuable, meaningful, expensive. Second, a $3 musical dustpan! Guess which one made the most points with me? The dustpan was related to my work and it tickled my fancy.

Any clever, unique novelty within the cleaning field will score points. There are toilet clocks, "mink" dustmop stoles, toilet-shaped erasers, and dozens of other related gifts you can consider.

Where do I find all this? I just keep my eyes and ears open; ideas are all over! With my constant use and flourishing of cleaning things, I can be the life of the party while helping to raise the visibility of our profession.

• Janus watches and other Janus items are available from PortionPac Chemical Corp. Write for a free brochure to:

PortionPac Chemical Corp.
400 North Ashland Ave
Chicago IL 60622-6382.

Cleaning Profession Catalog

You should find a price list inserted in the back of this book. Call right now to order any of the following cleaning novelties, 208-232-3535.

If the price list is missing, you can call for one, or send a POSTCARD with your name and address to:

Cleaning Profession Catalog
PO Box 700
Pocatello ID 83204.

Never lose your keys with this **Toilet Keyring**. Great reward for the kid who learns to clean.

Show pride in your profession by sporting a **Squeegee Lapel Pin.** It's a great reward for the window washer in training.

Toilet-shaped soup or hot chocolate mug leaves no doubt at break time as to who you are and what you do for a living.

Chocolate Outhouse! Make eye-catching centerpieces and inexpensive door prizes and decorations with this reusable candy outhouse mold.

Squirting Toilet I have one in my briefcase and I've even squirted governors, principals, and movie stars with it. Helps people realize that professional cleaners are people!

What do the first place winners get? The coveted **Golden Outhouse Trophy**. What better prize at your special event.

Always carry a **Johnny Lip Light** (to inspect under the rim of the toilet); playfully scare people with the idea that you're going to use it. "I'm as good as any dentist (we both work in enamels!)."

Found Tags to get those items safely back to their owners and let them know the names of the janitors that found them!

Colorful **Spot Removal Chart** makes a great giveaway for customers. Explains how to approach over 25 different stains.

Impressive, full color **Name Tags** that proclaim, "I am a Professional Cleaner." Actual size 3 7/8" x 2 5/8". Come in gangs of four to run through your printer, or hand letter. Designed to use with squeegee lapel pin.

Cleaning Clip Art Over 300 line drawings on one CD, from Don Aslett's own cartoonist. They'll bring to life your newsletters, flyers, cards, or brochures, anywhere you want or need a graphic depicting the greatest profession on earth.

10 Janitor Special Events

Ever heard of a **janitor ball?** A **janitor banquet?** How about a **janitor fashion show? Cleaning Olympics?** A **janitor rodeo?** No? Well, why not? The doctors have their get-togethers, the accountants, the schoolteachers. Why do all of them have group events and we the janitors just scrub away, is a good question! A few years ago, my company got tired of this second-rate treatment. Since there didn't seem to be any social happenings in our profession, we organized and held a few of our own. Our first was a genuine **Janitor Rodeo!** (See page 81.)

And did it ever go over! The TV show "Games People Play" flew in from California to film it. The next year, we hosted the world's first Janitor Fashion Show, and it, too, was an amazing success. We held it in a fancy hotel in Denver, and before we knew it, it was standing room only. During the Olympic year, we held the world's first Janitor Decathlon. Then we had a Janitor Opera complete with academy awards.

We've had such a good response to Janitor Special Events that I'm devoting an entire chapter of this book to them, so you can use and adapt them for your own purposes. They can spark up socials, conventions, parties, picnics, annual meetings, managerial get-togethers, and just about anywhere you assemble your people. Even training programs don't have to be 100% serious, long-faced sessions.

These events are designed so that everyone, staff and management, can participate along with spouses and families. Mix them all together and watch the love and goodwill that's transmitted.

Janitor Special Events are fun, but their real purpose is to instill a sense of pride and belonging, and enhance the self-image of the participants. They involve janitors and their families in an event that builds morale, binds their loyalty to the company, and brings them together as a group to reinforce a team spirit. It also gives them a chance to interact and communicate with owners, managers, supervisors, and administration away from the workplace—it can even improve relations with the boss when he gets out there and mixes in!

Nothing can beat a special event for creating good feelings, fun, and rejuvenation. It says to the public, "We exist!" It gives us a presence.

Janitor Special Events are also an especially good way to involve family and turn attitudes around. They give cleaners a chance to show off their skills, not just to coworkers and onlookers, but to spouses and children. They're also an excellent opportunity for families to find out first hand how many fine people are involved in the business.

The spirit of good-natured humor and enthusiasm will do a lot to create positive feelings and commitment to the company and to fellow employees. Breaking up the boredom and routine in your business and getting outsiders to look at it positively are the two

biggest things you can do to stimulate, encourage, and enthuse cleaning employees.

Create a sense of anticipation and competition in your own ranks, too. Have different cleaning departments, crews, floors, buildings, or divisions compete against each other and wear matching t-shirts specially produced for the occasion: Eighth Floor Dirty Dozen Wipes 'em Out. (See page 18.)

You already have most of the equipment you need for these events. The props and structures are all easy to build, and you have the talent and tools to do it right in your own cleaning ranks. Maintenance people will find these (and any other items you dream up) a whiz to make. If you want help, call me and we'll quote you a price to bring the props and put one on for you.

The following are the most popular events we've staged so far; I'm sure you'll be able to invent a few of your own and add to ours. The best part of a Janitor Special Event is that once you turn your people loose with the idea, their imaginations take off and they'll come up with a hundred fun ways to make it a success!

Don't Forget to Do Some Drum-Beating

Besides being a wonderful employee relations tool, Janitor Special Events are perfect media draws, and great opportunities to garner some much-needed publicity. Send press releases (samples follow) to newspapers, radio and TV stations two weeks before the

April 14, 1995

MARSH CREEK PRESS

A division of Don Aslett Inc.

FAX FLASH!

Aslett on Oprah Winfrey Show

Don Aslett, America's #1 Dejunker, will appear live from Chicago on the Oprah Winfrey Show this Thursday, **April 20, 1995** as part of a show titled "Time To Throw It Out!" He will be the expert guest on the show, helping packrats learn to dejunk their offices and homes and become more organized!

Don Aslett is author of *The Office Clutter Cure, Clutter's Last Stand, Not For Packrats Only* and other popular books on dejunking.

Aslett is owner of several companies including a contract cleaning firm, Varsity Contractors, Inc. operating in sixteen western states, The Cleaning Center and Marsh Creek Press both located in Pocatello, Idaho.

fax one page

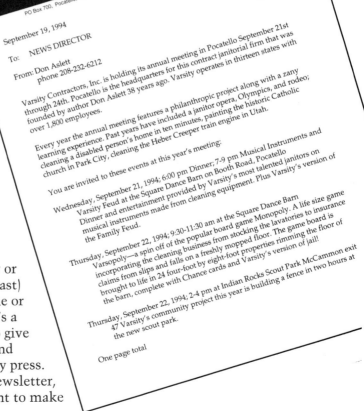

Don Aslett

PO Box 700, Pocatello, ID 83204 • Ph 208-232-6212 • Fx 208-232-6286

September 19, 1994

To: NEWS DIRECTOR

From: Don Aslett
      phone 208-232-6212

Varsity Contractors, Inc. is holding its annual meeting in Pocatello September 21st through 24th. Pocatello is the headquarters for this contract janitorial firm that was founded by author Don Aslett 38 years ago. Varsity operates in thirteen states with over 1,800 employees.

Every year the annual meeting features a philanthropic project along with a zany learning experience. Past years have included a janitor opera, Olympics, and rodeo; cleaning a disabled person's home in ten minutes, painting the historic Catholic church in Park City, cleaning the Heber Creeper train engine in Utah.

You are invited to these events at this year's meeting:

Wednesday, September 21, 1994; 6:00 pm Dinner; 7-9 pm Musical Instruments and Varsity Feud at the Square Dance Barn on Booth Road, Pocatello Dinner and entertainment provided by Varsity's most talented janitors on musical instruments made from cleaning equipment. Plus Varsity's version of the Family Feud.

Thursday, September 22, 1994; 9:30-11:30 am at the Square Dance Barn Varsopoly—a spin off of the popular board game Monopoly. A life size game incorporating the cleaning business from stocking the lavatories to insurance claims from slips and falls on a freshly mopped floor. The game board is brought to life in 24 four-foot by eight-foot properties rimming the floor of the barn, complete with Chance cards and Varsity's version of jail!

Thursday, September 22, 1994; 2-4 pm at Indian Rocks Scout Park McCammon exit 47 Varsity's community project this year is building a fence in two hours at the new scout park.

One page total

event. I've found them hungry for stories about real people like the janitors of the world. Don't be afraid to call and invite local celebrities like the mayor to attend your events. (They're always looking for a little publicity, too.) Publicity will up the maintenance department's status and visibility in the eyes of the company as a whole.

You can also write a story or feature on your coming (or past) event for a cleaning magazine or professional newsletter. If it's a **coming** event, you'll need to give them even more lead time and advance notice than the daily press. Don't forget the company newsletter, too, and you might even want to make up posters or flyers.

Assign a person in your company to be in charge of publicity. Have them maintain a list of local newspapers, magazines, radio and TV stations. Include on the list the mailing address, phone number, news director's name, and fax number for each. The handier information like this is, the better your chances will be of getting your info to the media and out in the public eye.

Page 78 shows a couple of press releases we faxed to the local press. Blanket all the media every time, and don't be disappointed if only one shows up—that's still a success!

Send press releases highlighting not only your Janitor Special Events but:

- Conventions, meetings, seminars
- Expansion or relocation
- New business
- New services or products
- Awards
- Contests within the company
- Speaking engagements
- New hires and promotions
- Employee news
- Professional organization news
- To promote events relating to our profession like National Housekeepers Week, Earth Day, or Chemical Safety Week

- Capitalize on current trends like recycling.

You can also get some "good press" by offering brief informational articles on cleaning (from the experts!) free to publications.

That All-Important Planning

- Let the head of the facility where you will hold the event know your needs way in advance.
- Draw a diagram to help you lay out your event.
- Determine how many helpers you will need, and train and coach them in advance.
- Find out if you'll need alternative materials for non-English speaking or reading participants.
- Be sure everyone way in the back of the room will be able to hear. Test any sound system in advance.
- Have some ways to involve members of the audience, to get things going, like front row awards.
- Plan to have pencils at the tables, masking tape to mark off the floor, etc.
- Allow room for spectators, friends, and family as well as other cleaners. Have plenty of chairs or a bleacher area.
- Set up early, so you're ready when the earlybirds arrive.
- Remind participants, SAFETY FIRST. No one has ever been hurt at any of our events, and you don't want anyone to be at yours, either!

JANITOR RODEO

Artie Johnson (remember him from "Laugh In"?) is the announcer: "Gentlemen, to your mounts... and they're out of the starting gate! First on the ground is the Urban Cowboy, quickly thrown off of Buffer's Choice. Now Clean Gene hangs on hard, going all out—the buzzer sounds—and the winner of the Buffer Brush Bronc Race is... Clean Gene Miller from Orofino, Idaho!"

That was the World's First Janitor Rodeo, back in 1979. It was covered by national media and featured on TV's "Games People Play." Since then the rodeo has been seen all over the continent, from Texas to British Columbia. Its popularity in the custodial community is unparalleled—where else can janitors compete in the things they do best?

Imagine the excitement of busting out of the gate and heading for the finish line alongside ol' Hop-a-long and Clean Gene in the **Buffer Brush Bronc Race!** Or how about pitting your custodial speed and skill against the last of the old-time cleaners in the **Cash-Box Key Race**? It's a good thing this is all in fun, pardner, the last hombre who lost this one is pushing up daisies on Boot Hill!

We all love a **Round-up**, but have you ever tried rounding up a balloon with a johnny mop and herding it through an opening in a toilet seat? It isn't easy, even without twenty other half-crazed janitors pushing and shoving to get there first. Or for real excitement, treat your trigger finger to an authentic Old-West shootout, the **Squirt-Bottle Fast Draw!** As you square off against your opponent, loosen up your "shooting" hand, lick your dry lips, and stay your jittery nerves. You're slinging cool water instead of hot lead—but the intensity's still there. The adrenaline's running and your heart leaps as Black Bart goes for his gun... you got 'em, right in the kisser! You'll never be the same again!

To bring people together for a great time, instill pride and let them know that the cleaning profession can be fun and rewarding, you can't beat a Janitor Rodeo. Here's how to make yours great:

First, janitorize it—decorate and dress the part! The rodeo theme should give you some great decorating ideas. Old milk cans, hay bales, and cardboard cutout cactus not only lend atmosphere—they can also be used in an obstacle course. Cowboy hats and country dress are a must, and I recommend Flatt and Scruggs (banjo and guitar) as background music. Janitorize right down to the munchies: a toilet punch bowl and mop bucket cupcakes, served on a dustpan!

The rodeo can be held in a gym or large meeting room—if the weather's good you can hold some events outside. Be sure there's room for a cheering section!

Make up scorecards (see p. 87) and rustle up family, friends, and extras to help with scoring and running the events. Some events can be done either as team, group, or individual competition. Scoring can be set up any way you like—we often give a certain number of points just for participating.

The events are fast-moving and require some real janitor know-how. If you think anyone can be a janitor, just try wrestling a 3-speed buffer, greenhorn! Here are some events that always make a big hit.

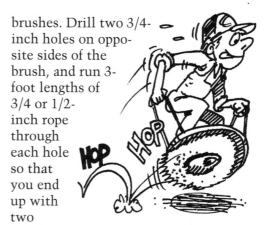

Barrel Racing (Brute style)**:** One cleaner steps inside a large wheeled garbage can and his partner, blindfolded, pushes the can along and navigates a course by listening to directions from the rider. This can be an obstacle course, where the Brutes have to work their way through desks, furniture, boxes, etc., to the dumpster, with demerits awarded for any obstacle hit; or it can be a timed race. Several Brutes can be going at one time, if there's room for some magnificent mass confusion. Watch that Brute bumping!

Buffer Brush Bronc Race: It's the old potato sack race, only using buffer brushes. Drill two 3/4-inch holes on opposite sides of the brush, and run 3-foot lengths of 3/4 or 1/2-inch rope through each hole so that you end up with two sturdy loops. Each contestant stands on a brush clutching the "reins" and hops to the finish (with some pretty interesting moves). A great way to use those old buffer brushes we all insist on keeping, "just in case." You can run this in heats of 6, and then have a final for the grand prize winner.

Uncovered Wagon Chariot Race: In a mop bucket, of course. The rider sits in a wheeled mop bucket any way he can and holds the head of a mop under each arm. The "horse" grabs the other ends of the two mops, and they're off racing around wet floor signs placed at 15-foot intervals. Make a few test runs to get the spacing right. Race the two wagons and eliminate the loser each time. There's bound to be a few spills, so keep it safe and sane.

Buffer Wrestling: Maneuver a buffer around an intriguing obstacle course. (Use your imagination to set one up.) If you've ever run one of these babies in a store, electronics plant, or anywhere there are breakables, you will appreciate the "bull in a china shop" feeling. It takes finesse to maneuver a buffer through the ins, outs, unders, arounds and throughs of the course without running into, spilling, or hitting anything. The cord can be a problem, so it's permissible for a friend to help control the cord.

Contestants have to first carefully back the buffer out of the "parking garage" (we use a large cardboard box with a buffer shape cut out of it—make it kind of a tight passage, even add a trip bell to the side to ring if they don't make it through clear). Then they have to pass through the pillars (plungers). Move the wastebasket from one side to another.

Weave in and out of the pylons (pop bottles with tennis balls on top, or wet floor signs). Now down the aisle (between two brooms), under the dust mop limbo stick, and back on home to the garage. Make the course spectacular and exciting. It'll drive the operator mad—to the delight of the friends and competitors.

Buffer Barrel Race: The winner is the one who makes the fastest time through a figure eight, or through a clover leaf pattern, without touching or knocking down the barrels, just as they do in regular barrel racing.

Bucking Buffer: This is kind of an urban cowboy event. Get a 19-inch buffer with a big motor. Put a 3M pad under it and then fold a thin pad three times and put it under one side so the buffer is off kilter and when running bucks or wobbles grotesquely. Give each contestant a cowboy hat and get the stopwatch ready. No holding onto anything. This is fast, exciting action—not for the fainthearted or easily bruised. The person who can stay on for the most seconds wins.

Squirt-Bottle Fast Draw: Good for the last event—everyone will love this one! Devise a couple of western-style holsters for spray bottles and fill the bottles with water. Then suspend a candle at chest height, out away from the body of each contestant. (You can do this on a frame made from a bent coat hanger.) Standing ten paces apart, opponents draw their weapons and try to shoot out each other's flame. It's wet and wild and great fun. You can play a little "The Good, the Bad, and the Ugly" or "High Noon" music for atmosphere and have someone drop a hanky for the starting signal. The real pros even spin their spray bottles. An alternate here is to have the "gunslingers" try to shoot blobs of whipped cream off each other's shoulders.

Out of the Chute: I've always sworn that people jump over floor mats—they'll often be clean when the ensuing floor is filthy. So how far can **you** leap over a mat? A 3-foot length is great for leaping over. Or use a 6-foot or longer runner for a standing long jump **on** to the mat.

Lasso Toss: Contestants try to

frisbee buffer pads into lariat circles on the floor (and you thought you'd finally get to rope a steer). Two or three ropes are made into different size circles with different scores assigned. Each contestant gets three 16" or 19" pads, and stands on the starting line, 30 feet away, and tries to land the pads clear inside.

The O.K. Corral: Teams race against the clock to put up aluminum scaffolding. Stop the clock when the whole team is atop its scaffolding. Appoint a "safety referee" to make sure no scaffold connections are slighted in the hustling.

Litter Lotto: Contestants take off their shoes, roll up their pant legs and put lightweight 30-gallon garbage cans over their heads. Then they pick up "trash" strewn all over the floor using toes only and lift it up to their hands. The trash is strips (about 2" x 6") of crepe paper—use different colors, and assign a certain number of points to each color. It's hilarious: hairy legs, clunking cans, wiggly toes.

Strongbox Key Race: Start out with a big ring of keys and a lot of different locks. Time contestants as they race to match the right key to the right lock. The one who finds the most right fits before the time is up, wins. (Old-time custodians who've had to handle a lot of keyrings will have a real edge here.)

84

We like to round out the rodeo with some tabletop events. These are great as fillers while participants are waiting to enter events. (See "The Cleaning Classic" for some less athletic but equally challenging activities that test other janitor skills.) And don't forget to award the winners with a little fanfare and ceremony! Whimsical gifts are guaranteed to bring a smile! The perfect prizes: A golden outhouse trophy, the coveted chocolate outhouse, a squeegee lapel pin, toilet key chain, toilet coffee mug, or squirting toilet. You might even give a Spot Removal Chart or other small treasure to every contestant. See page 76 for some possibilities here.

Following are some sample scorecard and setup ideas.

SAMPLE Preparation and Set-up

Place
We need a large room or gym indoors to hold the events.

Date • Time • Place
We have scheduled a **Janitor Rodeo** with your group on:

_____

at:

_____

location:

_____

We are anticipating approximately

_____ attendees.

The purpose of this event is:
• To provide a social, fun, group experience.
• To help train and motivate our cleaners.
• To gain publicity and recognition for your cleaning department.
• To say thank-you to and lift the image of your staff.

Size
Any number of participants from 25 to 250 works well. The more people, the tighter control you need.

Publicity
Alert all local TV, radio, and newspapers so they can cover the event. Arrange for one or more people to videotape and photograph the event for lasting value.

Prizes
Have a nice prize for the overall rodeo winner, and small prizes for individual events.

Decorations
Set a festive mood with western decorations and country music—encourage cowboy attire.

Audience
Invite family and friends as spectators to cheer and laugh. Set up chairs or a bleacher area.

Safety
Emphasize the need for safety—no one has ever been hurt in any of these competitions, let's keep it that way.

SAMPLE SCHEDULE

1:00pm Welcome/Rules
1:15pm Demo walk through
1:30pm Booths and events
           Challenge Tables
3:15pm General Assembly
           Champions
           Awards
           Drawings
4:15-4:30pm Closing ceremony

ADVANCE PREPARATION
Things to have on hand:

10 eight-foot tables for booth area
4 wheeled mop buckets (in good condition)
8 string mops with wood handles
3 upright vacuums in good working order
16" buffer with brush or polish pad
2 brutes with casters
1 case toilet paper (96 rolls)
Name tags
10 people to help at booths
Big prize for the Grand Prize Winner
2 extension cords
3 eighteen-inch scrub pads
microphone and sound system
4 wet floor signs
Scorecards

Props needed:

Signs and table drapes
Supplies and tools for each event
Small prizes/awards for each event
Guessing ballots
Booth displays
Decorations/flags
Starter gun for events

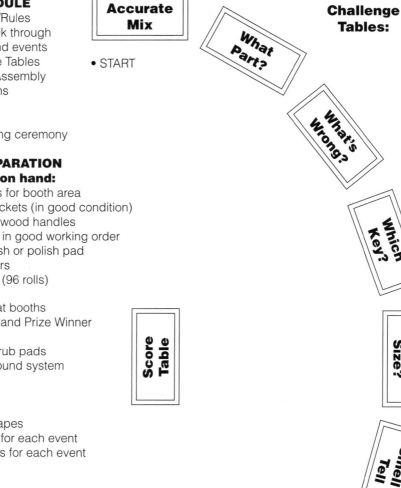

Accurate Mix

• START

Challenge Tables:

What Part?

What's Wrong?

Which Key?

Score Table

What Size?

Smell & Tell

Fast Draw

START!

Buffer Obstacle Course

NEED
Hard Floor
20' x 20'
Area

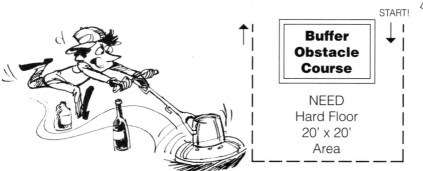

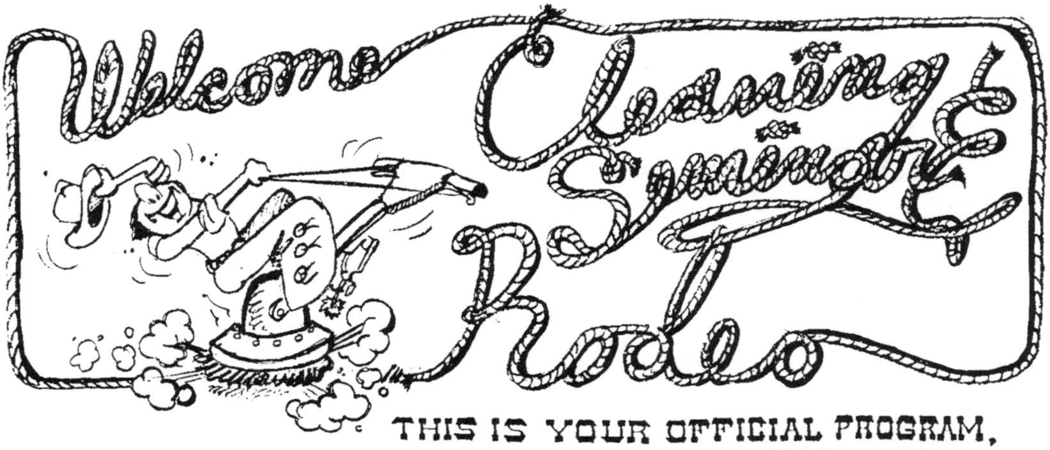

Welcome Cleaning Equipment Rodeo

THIS IS YOUR OFFICIAL PROGRAM, SCHEDULE, AND SCORECARD!

TIME-TABLE

Rodeo Held in the Morning:

8:30	General Assembly
8:45	Demo Walk Through
9:00	Booths and Events
11:00	General Assembly·
12:00	Closing / Awards-Drawing

Rodeo Held in the Afternoon:

1:00	General Assembly
1:15	Demo Walk Through
1:30	Booths and Events
3:30	General Assembly·
4:00	Closing / Awards-Drawing

HOW TO CLEAN A FLOOR!

Prepare your _____ and
 lotsunio

_____ the area and let it
 traustae

_____ for a long _____ .
 kaso   meti

When the _____ have
 hameclics

_____ the dirt, get an
 sidovels

_____ cloth and wipe.
 brostaben

The soil will nearly _____
 veerom

itself. The _____ it with
 erisn

water and _____ .
 valrten apso

SAFETY

USING AN EXTENSION LADDER:

Angle _____ foot

from the wall for every

4 feet of height.

Never stand on

the _____ rung!

5 points for each

correct answer.

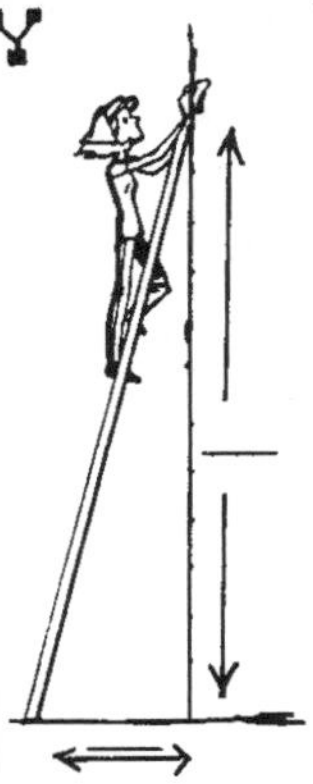

Record your score

THIS "JANITOR RODEO" IS BEING SPONSORED BY _____

Tally Up Your Score, Pardner

ACCURATE MIX:

Everyday we see "Dilute Concentrate 60-1, 20-1," etc. How much is 3 ounces? At table #1 take the red gallon jug and pour what you feel is 3 ounces into the bucket. Then check youself by pouring the contents of the bucket into the beaker. How did you do?

If you hit:

Right on.........10 points

Red line...........5 points

Yellow line........3 points

Record your score

WHAT PART?

Repairs often beat buying new tools. A working knowledge of parts is imperative. Can you recognize by feel only (and no peeking) what they are? Name and identify.

Each correct answer...3 points

1._____ 6._____

2._____ 7._____

3._____ 8._____

4._____ 9._____

5._____ 10._____

Record your score

WHICH KEY?

Start the stopwatch - pick up the ring of keys and unlock all items as fast as you can. Stop the watch at the end when you get the door open. How long did it take?

25 seconds (or less)....................20 pts.
25 to 40 seconds.........................15 pts.
40 to 60 seconds.........................10 pts.

60 to 90 seconds.......................5 pts.
over 90 seconds.........................1 pt.

Record your score

WHAT SIZE?

Judging right sizes to the right job saves time, money and you can do a better job. Stand back 3 feet and give an appraisal "size" and enter. NO COACHING!

1.   Mop_____oz
2.   Handle_____length

3.   Paint Roller_____in.
4.   Tape_____width
5.   Pipe_____diameter
6.   Wrench_____size
7.   Buffer Pad_____size
8.   Cleaner_____oz
9.   Container_____gal.
10   Squeegee_____size

3 points for each one you get right!

Record your score

SMELL AND TELL:

You can save a life, a floor, an explosion, by being able to identify the different cleaners, solvents, chemicals, food items, spots and stains. Sniff and write:

1._____ 6._____
2._____ 7._____
3._____ 8._____
4._____ 9._____
5._____ 10._____

3 points for each one you get right!

Record your score

BUFFER GOLF COURSE:

Can you run this floor machine with pin point accuracy? Now is your chance to find out. (A friend is allowed to hold the cord.)

Run through the buffer golf course. There are 30 pts. possible, 5 pts. maximum for each station. To start, guide buffer out between the bells, and to finish guide buffer back in. 5 pts. possible -1 for each touch of the bells. 5 pts. to push obstacle into the square - 4 if not placed. Hole in one 5 pts. - 2 pts. for hitting baseboard or extra try. In the hole 5 pts, rough 4 pts., sand 3 pts., water 2 pts. 5 pts to get through the fairway -1 for each ball knocked off. 5 pts. to clear sand traps - 2 pts. for each side default.

Record your score

Tally up both Rodeo *and* Skill events

FINAL SCORE

JANITOR CARNIVAL

This will be an easy one to do because we all have a store of memories about circuses and carnivals. For sideshows or booths, all you have to do is janitorize all the activities you once enjoyed as a child. For example, make your own version of these.

The Great Swami: Set up a table with a hole in the center and a fish bowl (crystal ball) over it and tell funny fortunes and tall tales. Have a light and helper under the table to help with sound effects and supernatural happenings.

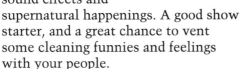

A good show starter, and a great chance to vent some cleaning funnies and feelings with your people.

Bowl Swab Throw: Outline a figure with Velcro on a sheet of plywood. Make the strips at least 2 inches wide, in different colors and assign a different score to each color. Contestants throw bowl swabs (like knives) which will stick to the Velcro. High score wins; hit the figure inside and you

have to donate a quarter to the janitor picnic fund.

Ring the Bell: Not only for the strong! Contestants see if they can thrust a toilet plunger with enough force to ring the bell! You can construct one of these with things you have around. Mark the lower end of the scale with things like "phew," or "loser," and write "Winner" big and bold at the top.

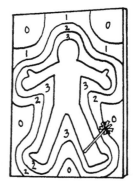

Janitor Museum or Freak Show: A glass display case of novelties: incredibly worn vacuum parts (or the strangest thing ever picked up by a vacuum), largest dust ball ever encountered, the most amazingly clean mop water, company uniform that's seen the most wear, raggety-est rag, rare and exotic pieces of equipment (identify each with a little explanation), etc.

Outhouse Throw: Why aim at a bullseye or beanbag when you can nail the real thing—a colleague, a friend, the boss! Small wet sponges make a big smack and splash and hurt no one. Build a one or two holer. Arrange it so that the heads stick up through the seats to dodge and taunt, while contestants try for a "head-on" hit at three sponges per try.

Wheel of Fortune: Take an old (or new) 22-inch buffer brush, and mount it on a 24"x 6" piece of 3/4" plywood. Mount it on a simple wheel bearing so it will spin, add a bunch of short pieces of 1/2" dowel and a plastic flipper. This will give you everything you need to spin the Wheel of Fortune to predict fortunes, win awards and prizes, etc. You might even

clip a $100 or $50 bill in one of the spaces. No matter which employee gets it, they'll all love it.

Weight Guessing Booth: Touchy, but **fun!** If the official guesser misses by more than ten pounds the employee (weighee) wins a prize. A dinner pass or gift certificate to an inexpensive restaurant is a great prize here.

B.B. Gun Pad Shoot: Put small balloons in the center of buffer pads mounted on a bearing so that they'll spin. Assign scores to the balloons according to color—red 10; white 5; etc. Make sure there is a large, well-padded backdrop behind the target area, so that the b.b.'s don't bounce, and even bad shots can't stray out of the area.

The Juggler: Every carnival needs a juggler. One of your more dexterous dirt chasers can juggle toilet rolls, soap bottles, or anything janitorial.

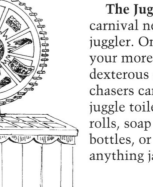

CARNIVAL SCORE-CARD

NAME_____

Hand your score card to the "booth barker" and he/she will record your score --
be sure to remind him/her to give you 3 points for participating in the event.
Scores cannot be changed later.

POINTS

☐ Vacuum Belt Volley Three tosses: 1st ringer=5; 2nd=10; 3rd=15.

☐ As the Buffer Turns Three spins; Points given for each spin.

☐ Toilet Man Toss Three tosses; Score for each toss.

☐ Guess Your Weight Miss by 10lbs=5; miss by 20lbs=10; miss by 30lbs=15.

☐ Shoot the Moon 1st hit=5; 2nd hit=10; 3rd hit=15.

☐ Brute Push Complete course hitting no barriers=20; hit 1 barrier=15; hit 2=10. For completing course=5 points.

☐ Buffer Pad Pop 6 shots, 5 points per popped balloon.

☐ Pitch in Porcelain

☐ Tissue Stacking Mania HEIGHT_____ Top 3 stackers=30, 20, 10 points.

☐ How Fast Can You Load the Van? TIME_____ Three fastest times=30, 20, 10 points.

☐ Extra Points Back of card must be complete, see below.

☐ **TOTAL POINTS**

Total your score and turn in this card to
Arlo Luke to be eligible for prizes at the
end of the evening.

15 Extra Points given for writing your
most embarrassing moment on the back
of this score card.

*This is to certify that I have, to be best of my ability, entered each of the
above events with the vigor and enthusiasm of a Varsity Janitor.*

Signed_____

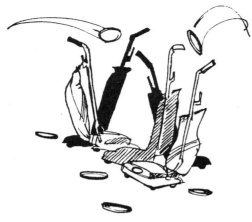

Vacuum Belt Ring Toss: Round up your upright vacs (you might even paint some old junkers a classy carnival red) and put them about eight feet away. Give each contestant five vacuum belts to try and toss over the handles. Have one vacuum (the jackpot model) alone and further back with a big prize.

Mop Bucket Merry-Go-Round: A

few plumbing pipes with mop buckets balanced on the end of the arms makes a great target for wet sponges. Then the "Merry-Go-Round" can be turned by motor, or by hand. Give a tiny prize for getting one sponge in, and a **grand prize** for plunking a sponge into all four buckets.

Dunk the Boss: Provide a simple cheap toilet for a seat, with an elevated, light plastic flush tank above it, with the drain valve directly above the head of the contestant. Each participant gets three throws of a wet sponge

to hit a bullseye set up on the flush tank. If the thrower misses then he has to trade places with the hot seat. This goes on until somebody gets wet (provide a shower cap for the ladies).

The Cleaning Classic

This is a fun tournament of skills and cleaning adventures made into competitive games and contests.

Blind Window Squeegee: hang up a piece of thin metal about the size of a window (2'x3') and place 5 little magnets all over it. Blindfolded, the contestant tries to clean all the magnets into one corner, using proper squeegee technique (a fanning motion). They only get one try.

What's In There? Take a sheet of 1/2-inch plywood and cut a dozen 6-inch holes with a sabre saw. Attach a small cloth bag to each hole from the behind. Place a cleaning object in each one of the bags (parts, fuses, tools) that every janitor should be familiar with. Then have contestants feel (because they can't

see) and tell what's in there. **Great fun!** It really embarrasses some bosses when the crew beats them.

This can also be done with draw-string bags that contestants can stick their hands in.

Measuring Up: Every day we read "Dilute Concentrate 60:1," or 20:1, etc. Our estimating skills are always in action, and here's a chance to put  them to the test. Can they measure out an ounce by sight? At this table have a gallon of red-colored water and have each contestant pour what he or she feels is an ounce of it into a bucket. Then they score themselves for accuracy by pouring the bucket into a beaker. (This one can help save hundreds of gallons of cleaning chemicals in the future.)

What Part?: Repairing often beats buying new tools. A working knowledge of parts is important to a janitor. Ten parts from different pieces of cleaning equipment are concealed inside a cloth or paper bag. Contestants try to identify them by feel alone (no peeking).

What Size?: Being able to pick the right size for the job saves time and money. (For this test of sizing skill, have the following articles—or others—sitting back 3 feet from the table.) Contestants have to estimate the size of each thing—no coaching!

1. Mop Head _____ oz.
2. Mop Handle _____ length.
3. Paint Roller _____ inches.
4. Tape _____ width.
5. Pipe _____ diameter.
6. Wrench _____ size.
7. Buffer Pad _____ size.
8. Jug of Cleaner Concentrate _____ oz.
9. Bucket _____ gal.
10. Squeegee _____ inches.

Janitor Closet Inventory : A large pile of cleaning supplies, tools and chemicals are heaped out of sight. Then the names of the items are written on slips of paper and placed in large box ("the janitor closet"). Each team member in turn then draws a piece of paper and yells out the name of the item. Then he runs to the pile, finds the item and packs it back to the "closet." Then he tags the next team member who draws, yells out the item and goes for it. The first team to get the designated number of items (about 5) into their closet wins. Make sure the pile is all mixed up and has a few extra things tossed in to confuse the hunters, such as the wrong sizes. For example, have one paper that says 14-inch buffer pad, and have an 18- or 16-inch one in there too to keep them on their toes.

The Mat March (the janitor version of musical chairs): Spread a number of small 1' x 1' mat pieces (or carpet squares with rubber backs, so they won't slip) close together in a circle. When the music stops, everybody

scrambles to a mat, to avoid being eliminated. Remove one mat each time you stop the music. Do this to the music of "Irish Washerwoman" or other appropriate tunes. This is a **great** social mixer.

What's Wrong With It? Take an ordinary vacuum and make a half-dozen or so things wrong with it: clip the bag upside down, put the belt on backwards, see that it has a frayed cord, ground plug missing, missing beater, bumper, etc. Then set it on display and let each contestant look it over carefully and see how many of the six or eight problems they can find. Great challenge and great training.

The Wall Wash (Wipeout?): With spray bottle and cloth have the contestants run (to get them out of breath) over to a 4' x 8' sheet of plastic laminate well smeared with dirt and wash it. Or you can show them the real professional way to clean walls (see *Is There Life After Housework?* Chapter 15), arm them with sponges and buckets, and see who brings back the cleanest water! Make this a time trial, or judged by the cleanness of the wall.

Smell and Tell: A janitor can save a carpet, a life, an explosion—just by being able to identify different cleaners, solvents, chemicals, spots and stains. Have the following items—or others—in numbered salt shakers (opaque ones, so they can't be seen through): ammonia, vinegar, Ben Gay, floor wax, bleach, ketchup, mustard, paint thinner, coffee, cigarette butts, window cleaner. Contestants carefully sniff each container and then write their guess. Points for each correct answer.

Roll Up the Hose: Stretch out two 60-80 ft. lengths of light hose and at the signal GO, each team (which can be composed of two crew members, or a couple) tries to roll up a hose more neatly than their foe. Winners eliminate each other until a champion hose roller is found.

Vacuum Assembly Contest: Take three standard upright vacuums and take the bags off, the beater bars out, the plates off, the belts off, undo the cords and leave all the pieces of each vacuum in a neat pile. At the other end of the room, put three piles of soda cracker crumbs and three teams of two. At the word GO, the first to get the vacuum assembled and the crumbs all vacuumed up, is the winner! Have one team of bosses (they get skunked all the time and the crews love it, talk about enthusiasm).

The Slippery Floor: (An outside event, for obvious reasons.) Everyone, sometime in their cleaning life, wonders what it would be like to run and dive across a clean soapy floor. At last, a chance to work it all out. Get a heavy piece of clear plastic (2 mil., if possible, so it won't snag) 50 feet long. Lay it out on the grass and anchor the plastic at the corners in a way that doesn't leave anything sharp sticking up for anyone to run into. Then get a hose and wet the plastic down well. All that's left is the event itself! Contestants can dive feet first, head first, or seat first from a running start to see who goes the farthest. It's hard to get hurt on the smooth slippery surface and the action is hilariously funny. (It will separate the brave, gutsy cleaners from the chickenhearts.)

Janitor Olympics

Perfect for the Olympic Year. This is like the Janitor Rodeo, you simply janitorize a series of Olympic events. For awards we spray paint putty chisels bronze, silver and gold.

The identifying focal point of the Olympics is the famous torch being passed from runner to runner. As janitors we have the perfect tool to emulate the torch—a bowl swab (flaming or not).

Extension Pole Vault: Using an extension pole or a 72-inch mop handle, after a running start the contestants propel themselves as far across a line drawn on the ground as they can, and land on an old mattress. You could also work out a variation on this in which entrants have to vault over a stack of paper towels.

Toilet Seat Skateboard Race: A little more dangerous than cleaning the toilet, but lots more fun. Mount some rubber casters firmly on the bottom of an old toilet lid (three wheels are easier to ride). Make several of these so that you can get a race going. Get someone to pull or a slight hill to speed things up. The "skateboards" can be decorated in authentic Indy or dragster style.

Bowl Brush Soccer:
Everyone enjoys this one. Blow up balloons until they're about six inches around and tie. Give each contestant a bowl swab and have them all line up. On the signal "GO" they try to be the first to bat and coax their balloon across the room or field and

through the toilet seat which is held open at the finish line. What a delightful mass of swinging bowl brushes, banging balloons and frustrated people. Even the kids can enter this one. We usually stage three separate heats: men, women and kids, then have the three winners race in the final. Boy do the men and women get competitive (no fist fights yet, just snarls). The kids generally beat them both.

filled balloons, tosses them over the net as far as she can. The other partner, armed with a small plastic bucket or a mini toilet, attempts to catch them. Some folks can really sling the balloons and that calls for some fast footwork by the "catcher." The balloon caught the farthest distance from the net wins.

Bucket Rowing Races:
Anyone can do it! On a hard or soft surface floor, each cleaning athlete sits (or kneels or perches any way he can) in a large wheeled mop bucket. Using two toilet plungers as oars—on your mark, get set, "GO!"—they try to out-row the other race entries from one end of the

room to the other. The plungers slip and slide and sometimes stick to the floor, swinging the driver around in circles. It's hilarious! Little guys can beat the big guys easily in this one.

Toilet Volleyball: (An outdoor event.) Partners, or couples, such as husband and wife, get on the opposite side of a volleyball net and one member of the team, armed with water-

Push Broom Prowess (Relay Race): Just how good and fast are you and your crew with a plain old push broom? Now's the time to find out! The only equipment you need is an 18-inch push or street broom and a miniature football. As in all relay games you have to take into account the size of the room and the number of people involved. Have five-member teams push the little football around a course, through a goal and back. Or set up a circular course and hand off the broom like a baton. Be ready for a lot of cheering and pandemonium.

Plunger Flip: Each of the eight or ten participants lines up with a vacuum belt and a plunger that will stick to a hard-surface floor. (The plungers need to have a small notch cut in the handle, near the top.) The plungers are stuck firmly to the floor, and at the signal "GO," contestants loop the belt over the handle of the plunger, into the notch, pull the belt back slingshot style, and let fly. Wherever the belt lands is where the contestant runs to, smacks the plunger down, and repeats the action. The first person to get all the way up the floor and back is the winner.

Mop Wringing Relay: For this you just need a bucket of plain water, a wringer or cone mop bucket, and a small mop. The first person to get all the water transferred from the bucket to the mop bucket (using only the mop and wringer)—and mop the floor, is the winner. There are endless variations on this one, like handing the mop down a line, or having a big tub of water and the winner is the first one who gets their mop bucket full using only their mop and wringer—and no spilling! Be careful of slipping on the wet floor.

Standing Mat Jump: One of the most basic of all athletic events is the standing broad jump. It's a simple matter to convert it to a Standing Mat Jump. This has always been a favorite of mine. I know the skills for it exist, because for years I've noticed that the long doormat runner at the entrance to a building will often stay perfectly clean while the first few feet of flooring are total grit and grime.

Carpet-covered, rubber-backed door mats are the only equipment you need for this game. A 4'x8' mat is the perfect size, most people will jump between 50 and 80 inches. Have the competitors put the tips of their toes on the edge of the mat and leap as far forward as they can. Measure and mark the mat with a piece of chalk where the back of the heel hit, or if they fall back on their hands, mark and measure that as their score. In this event it's a good idea to have separate male and female divisions. A jackrabbit from Brown University in Rhode Island has the world record of 87 inches; if you beat that, give me a call and I'll enter your name in the Janitor Book of Records.

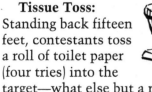

Tissue Toss: Standing back fifteen feet, contestants toss a roll of toilet paper (four tries) into the target—what else but a real toilet!

Janitor Gym or Janigames

Come up with a series of events and activities to take off on the ever-popular indoor fitness activities, such as:

- a buffer bench press
- weight lifting (with a set of dumbbells made from two 5-gallon cans and a broom handle)
- a mop bucket/plunger rowing machine
- plunger isometrics
- cleaning routine aerobics
- ankle and wrist exercise or jogging

weights made from PortionPac cleaners.

Safety Rally

At one of our company meetings we held a Safety Rally (or Safety Rodeo). The events targeted issues like proper lifting technique, the right way to back up trailers, vehicle safety, loading and unloading tools, boxes, and equipment, scaffolding setup, and safe chemical handling. Here's an example:

Load: You are a supervisor, and have received a call from one of your most valuable customers. They need a job done immediately. You have only 15 minutes until you have to be on the job and it takes 10 minutes to drive there. You and your entire crew must load everything into the truck, secure it, and be ready to leave within 4 minutes.

Off-duty state policemen were the judges and handed out citations for safety infractions.

Pom-Pom Girls

What do you get when you reverse Pom-Pom Girls? Mop-Mop Girls. Who better to cheer on your games?

Team Events

Most events can be adapted for individual or team play, here are some examples.

Sponge throw: each team is allowed to pick one member of the firm to be in the stocks. Each team member is allowed two attempts to hit the target with a water-soaked sponge. Five points for a direct hit in the head, two points for a hand hit.

Mop wringer relay: teams saturate mop in a bucket full of water and run to an empty bucket with a cone wringer. The first team to fill their bucket wins.

A Main Event

You don't want to be without a big **Main Event.** If Evel Knievel can leap 20 motorcycles, then by George one of your greats can do something spectacular, too, such as leap 100 rolls of toilet paper in a single bound. One time the president of our company made the jump down a big slide, over a tower of toilet tissue, into a swimming pool. What a way to top off an evening, either a wipe out or a clean sweep! Have a drum roll and all the dramatic preliminaries. Your hero can dress in skin-tight pants with a crash helmet and all the trimmings. What a way to go—think up a **Main Event** to fit your occasion!

Janitor Fashion Show

Our maids are better looking than most models anyway, and so are our janitors. This is an inexpensive and relatively easy activity to pull off, especially if you assign each person, group, company, or crew one particular fashion or type of outfit to wear. The rules are that all apparel must be made out of cleaning materials or cleaning tools. My wife and I often go as Mr. and Mrs. Toilet. I carry my toilet suitcase and wear pumice stone cuff links and a dust rag tie. On one of these occasions my wife got a giant buffer brush and cut the center of it out so she could slip it over her hips like a miniskirt. The bristles of the brush were a little short, so she hung some mopstrings (quite becoming, really) down off it too. But to get her to wear two toilet plungers for the top half took some real talking!

We wrote a script for the entire show to match the fashion shows you've seen on TV. You can do it, too! All you need is some modeling music and a long stage, then each entry waltzes out to the music as the soft voice of the narrator describes the apparel, just as in the finest Parisian show. A trip to the mall or the department store will show you what you need to imitate. Your fashions could hardly be any more incongruent or exaggerated than what you see there. It will be funny and wild! The spectators will enjoy it as much as the participants.

Evening Gown: Our cleaning company President's wife appeared in a gown of laundry bags with a bonnet buffer hat, SOS pad earrings, and a 36-inch dust mop head wrapped around her shoulders like a magnificent ermine stole. Everything she wore was cleaning oriented. She moved and paced to the music and the crowd loved it.

Red Hot Stripper: As raucous "stripper" music blares away, one of our crew comes on stage in a bright orange poncho, and at the climactic moment whips it off to reveal shorts and big floor stripping boots, etc.

Pumice Shoe Cowboy: Here comes a janitor in the biggest, best western getup you've every seen; buffer pad chaps, dustpan spurs, crisscrossing ammo holder filled with pumice stones (Rambo style), and more.

Pantomime: Two cleaners did a pantomime of cleaning a building, then toasted the accomplishment with entwining toilet plunger goblets filled with bubbly 7-Up. Another couple modeled undies completely made of trash bags (using liners and the lot)—they didn't look bad either.

You can add a few specialty characters and costumes too, to spice up the show, such as: Super Janitor, Anti-compliant Suit, OSHA Cleaner Attire.

Janitor Talent Show

Holding a crew or company talent show with hilarious skits will be one of the most satisfying events you ever have. And it'll inspire and motivate your people more than you can imagine.

At first, the very thought of this may terrify your workers—even the boss. The idea of getting up in front of the crowd and performing scares us all. **Do it anyway!** You'll be surprised at the talent that emerges. Down deep we all have talents—often more than one, whether or not they've ever been fully developed. We can all dance, sing, do dramatic readings, magic tricks, skits, or perform in some way—we can all do something.

As bosses and owners and managers we probably feel we really know our maintenance people, but to our surprise we may find that our janitors are accomplished violinists, singers,

artists, gourmet cooks, seamstresses, etc. The chance to make your talents known in public is everyone's secret wish—even the most bashful.

Tell your people that they can do anything as long as it has a janitorial theme. Give them a time limit of 2 to 5 minutes. Any funny experiences, gripes, or mishaps that happen in and around the janitor scene can be turned into funny pantomimes. Making fun of the boss or supervisor is always good for bringing down the house.

One of our most stage-shy managers finally agreed to do a skit of the boss trying to explain some work to be done to a Spanish-speaking employee who, as the humorous conversation would lead you to believe, didn't understand English. At the end of the skit the boss, totally undone from his efforts to communicate, gave the worker his paycheck. The South of the Border sweeper took one look at it and in perfect English, hollered that he'd been shortchanged on his payroll deductions. The house broke into laughter and applause.

In every group there are some truly funny would-be comedians. Appoint them as master of ceremonies and let them play it up good. Who knows, the best skit or drama may come from the purchasing office or one of your invited guests.

Be sure to videotape your show so you can play it back and get continued mileage.

Janitor Opera/Musical

From *Oklahoma* to the *Sound of Music*, we each have our favorite musical. Substitute a plot that involves a cleaning situation and ask each crew member to contribute a verse, scene, lip sync, or adaptation. "Yankee Doodle" to "Three Blind Mice," "Please Release Me" to "Chattanooga Choo Choo," "I'm Cleaning for a White Christmas," or the "Twelve Days of Cleaning." You could even include—imagine—a mop chorus line. When we staged our first janitor musical we were all shocked to find out how many in our ranks could play an instrument, sing, dance, act, and perform.

Janitor Band (Sounds Good, Too!)

At our annual company meeting, we always have a "make it out of cleaning tools" contest. You've read about our mailboxes, vac animals, mop creations, etc. Several years ago we asked our cleaners for musical instruments made from cleaning paraphernalia—instruments that would actually work, make music! Not only did they make the instruments, at the first evening social of the meeting, each entrant demonstrated his entry in action.

It was amazing what we cleaning people came up with. There were

harps made out of dustpans, trombones made out of backpack vacs and squeegees, and lots of stringed instruments such as a mandolin made out of an upright vac. They put keyboards on floor scrubbers and one was mounted on the back of a real china toilet.

Our CEO, Arlo Luke, was a viola player in the city symphony. He put a set of strings on a hardbox vacuum and made a cello that sounded like the real thing, even played a few licks on it!

Our California district (you know how those Californians are) put their instruments together into a western band. They had drums made out of a wet/dry vac and upturned Brutes and trash cans, a buffer guitar, and a keyboard mounted in a Clarke floor scrubber with speakers built into it. They not only thrilled us, but were asked to play in the main lobby of the MGM Grand Hotel in Las Vegas for the 10,000+ who came to the Building Service Contractors convention. Here's a sampling of the lyrics they janitorized. A great way to help uplift our image and provide group bonding and team building power for the betterment of cleaning.

Mamas, Don't Let Your Babies Grow Up to Be Cleaners

Mamas, don't let your babies grow up to be cleaners,
Let 'em be plumbers, or drive an ol' truck,
Let 'em be locksmiths, kill insects or such.

Mamas, don't let your babies grow up to be cleaners,
Their hands always reek and they look like a geek
Even to someone they love.

Cleaners love moldy old bathrooms and tripe covered dumpsters, worn out ol' vacuums, and key rings, and pants that fit tight.
Them that don't know him, don't want to, and them that do mostly just try to avoid him. His hands ain't dirty, but who knows where he's been or what he's been into tonight…

Help Me Make It Through the Night

Take this mop here from my hand
Shake it lose and let it fall
Lay it flat against the floor
Don't get the wax upon the wall
Come and wax here by my side
Til the early mornin' light
All I'm askin' is your time
Help me make it through the night
I don't care what's right or wrong
You don't have to understand
Get your foot out of that bucket
Get over here'n give me a hand…

It's all in fun, of course, but activities like these send a message loud and clear to outsiders who don't appreciate cleaners, that we are not only smart, we're talented, and we know how to enjoy ourselves.

Parades

How many janitors have you ever seen in a parade? None! What's wrong with us? Ashamed? Too bashful? Too lazy? Nothing to parade? Or none of the above?

We have every good reason to enter and participate in parades. What better time and place to let the world know that we exist? Why not join in and help bring a spark to any parade—city, county, school, homecoming, Fourth of July, or other holiday. Think up a clever cleaning act and come behind the parade. You'll advertise your company and your job and have fun doing it.

Our company, for example, turned a child's miniature truck into a company truck and lettered it just like our big ones. On parade day we follow the troops, armed with scoops and brooms to clean up the debris and horse droppings. Guess what part of the parade gets the most applause and appreciation? If you don't have a mini car you can use a wagon, a big wet-dry vacuum, or a decorated wheelbarrow. As you and your crew clean up those "parade biscuits," have one person spray aerosol deodorant on the spot afterwards. Others can run to the edge of the parade and tease and please the crowd , collect trash, etc. When the parade stops for a minute, set up a squirt bottle fast draw shootout with holstered spray bottles. Or do a short chorus line with shovels and brooms—

even hand out printed flyers with cleaning secrets, compliments of your professional staff. You and your crew can come up with a million laughs.

To enter most parades you just call the parade chairman well in advance and tell him or her what you have in mind and what you're going to do. Make sure you don't conflict with other marching groups or act in any way offensive to the crowd. The chairman should be more than pleased to have a cleanup crew that also adds color to the parade. Get as many of your people to participate as you can.

As to just what you might **do** in the parade, here's a few more ideas you might like:

• The intellectual outhouse: Have one person inside a portable outhouse (motorized or foot powered) talking to the public, answering cleaning questions, etc.

• Floats: display new equipment or how to do certain jobs, like window cleaning, on a moving float to draw wows and applause.

• A janitor band: Convert cleaning equipment (you can exercise a lot of imagination here) into some musical instruments to play as you march along.

• March a mop-wielding drill team in white gloves with a plunger-twirling baton leader. Add a band with a garbage-can bass drum, vacuum hose tuba, and trash can lid cymbals.

• String out on the route the world's largest roll of toilet paper (one of the new super rolls). Make sure the crew polices it all up afterward, too, of course.

• Push "Miss Latrine Queen" (one of your janitors, rigged up in a humorous "janitor glamor" costume) along on a janitor cart as your entry to the parade beauty pageant.

• Use buffer brushes to cover the wheels of a cart and make it into a janitormobile.

• Attach large cardboard cutouts to each side of small motor bikes to make them look like large toilets and have employees drive them towing mop buckets. Or turn your pickup into a toilet.

• A squadron of five or six toilet seat skateboarders (see page 95).

Here's some of the literature my company uses to plan and promote parades.

Attention: Varsity Managers
Subject: Varsity Parade Kit

OBJECTIVE: Being recognized and remembered by people in your community is a key principle in selling new business. Many people have a negative view of the cleaning business, so anything you can do to portray it in a fun, positive light will be enjoyed and remembered. The Varsity Parade Packet gives you everything you need to be the highlight and the most-remembered entry in your town's next parade. All the directions are here, plus all the equipment and clothing you need to make it a success.

1. Parade Qualification. First check with your Chamber of Commerce to see what parades are held in your city, and who to contact. The big parades require entries to be registered months in advance, so make sure you plan far enough ahead. Check with the parade committee to make sure you qualify—some parades permit absolutely no commercialization, some are more permissive about displaying company names and slogans, etc.

2. Reserve a Parade Kit. Let the home office know when you need the Parade Kit and reserve it as far ahead as possible. Allow ten days for delivery, and give us an estimate of how many toilet novelty items you will need. Home office pays the freight to you, your only expense is freight back and whatever novelties you use.

3. Give the parade committee one of the enclosed brochures, "Our Parade Entry," so they will know exactly what you are planning. Make sure they know that you need to come near the end of the parade to be effective.

4. When you get the kit you will find:
   • A little Varsity pickup, which is pushed like a wheelbarrow.
   • Two toy shovels and brooms
   • Four White Varsity jumpsuits— 2 medium, 2 large (notice that they are clean, please return them that way)
   • Two spray bottle holsters
   • Whatever novelty items you order
   You supply your own spray bottles, window cleaning equipment, and whatever other gear you plan to use.

5. In the parade. Be sure to use people with good personalities and a sense of humor—they must be able to ham it up and have a good time with the crowd. Just follow the parade, scooping and picking up any litter, leaving the street nice and clean. Follow the suggestions for "Crowd Pleasers" or make up some of your own!

6. Publicity. Be certain to have someone take photos for your own files, and for you to submit to the media. Let the newspapers know what you are doing ahead so they can be prepared for good coverage. Try to find out where their photographer is, so you can do something particularly funny for a good news photo.

7. After the parade. Clean up the props and carefully pack them for shipping back to the home office. Don't delay as someone else may be waiting for them.

VARSITY PARADE SKIT CROWD PLEASERS

When you do the parade skit, half the fun and benefit is interaction with the crowd. Be sure to use people in the parade who have personality, and who are not afraid to ham it up. Here are some ideas to make it fun, and add your own:

1. Throw out toilet erasers, and maybe some toilet keychains, toilet earrings, etc. to people in the crowd.

2. Have a squirting toilet to spray selected spectators. (Be careful who you squirt—not everyone will think this is funny.)

3. Tidy up selected spectators—dust off hat, brush lint off clothes, polish shoes, etc.

4. When parade stops, set up a squirt bottle fast-draw shootout, either with your own crew or with someone from the crowd. (Water only please.)

5. When stopped, grab window washing gear out of the truck, and run over and wash the windows on a nearby storefront.

6. Have your crew do a chorus line routine with shovels and brooms.

7. Ham it up when you clean up the parade litter—plant and pretend to find bizarre items (a pair of false teeth and try to find the owner in the crowd, etc.). Have a spray bottle to disinfect and deodorize the horse droppings when you scoop them up.

VARSITY CONTRACTORS

OUR
PARADE ENTRY

As the nation's most colorful cleaning company, we like to practice what we preach—that is making the world a cleaner place! Our parade entry is a cute little cleaning truck which is pushed like a wheelbarrow or street sweeping cart. We come at the end of the parade, after all the other entries have gone by, to clean up! Our sharp, uniformed cleaning crew will police up all of the torn crepe paper, pop cans and candy wrappers, clean up and deodorize the horse apples, and generally take care of any parade litter. We will leave the parade route spiffed up and sparkling!

To be effective, we will need to be at the end of the parade, where we can pick up after everyone ahead of us. We have several novelty items, such as toilet-shaped pencil erasers, which we like to toss out to the crowd, if that is permitted. Our little truck has a company logo on it which says <u>Varsity Contractors, Inc.</u>, and each crew member has a <u>Varsity</u> patch on his uniform. Other than that, there is no commercialization of our entry.

For further information, contact:

Name _____

Address _____

City _____ State ____ Zip _____

Telephone ( ) _____

Even More Ideas for Cleaning Get-Togethers

Cleaning companies, crews, and associations find many occasions to gather: training sessions, organization meetings, luncheons, awards, annual meetings, trade shows, etc. Spice them up with a special activity or theme. Here are some that have worked well!

Break Entertainment

As a break in a long meeting or to spark up a training session, there are yet other "janitor exhibitions" you can use to inspire your crews.

Dustmop Shuffleboard: This is just like real hotel and ocean liner shuffleboard except you use a dustmop (preferably a 24-inch or smaller). The "puck" is a small 3M nylon floor machine scrubbing pad and you use masking tape to set up a scoring area on a hard floor with a variety of preassigned scores. Each challenger, with a thrust of the mop, attempts to place the puck in the scoring zone. This is a milder game than most and can be enjoyed as a side activity on a more sedate schedule of events, or is a good choice for a less physically active group of cleaners. You can make the course short or long to fit the size of the facility and the energy of the personnel.

Which brings us to the **Dustmop Shuffle:**

Just moppin' along,
I'll be here all night,
the room's a mess,
hey what a sight;
you see I got this job,
and I do it slick,
the boss he taught me every trick.
No, it ain't no trouble;
just watch me do

the dustmop shuffle.

Surely a member of your crew can rap better than this. In no time at all I bet you'll have a hit.

Commode Camelot: During a short break, two of our more athletic cleaning heros put on a display of knightly skill and valor in a little toilet plunger tournament. Each of the opponents wields a toilet plunger "sword," and garbage can lid shield. A handkerchief is dropped and the duel begins. A little chalk or powder on the lip of the plunger clearly reveals when a "sword" has struck home. (Admittedly this one is not so much a display of skill as pure entertainment.) Names like "Duke of the Dustpan" or the "Knightroyal Flush" add spice to the match.

The Dung Fu Kid: One of the best cleaning skits I've every seen was performed by a young Coast Guardsman who entered the stage dressed in a white Kung Fu ghee. He was loudly introduced as the Dung Fu Kid. With a toilet plunger (for a samurai sword) in each black-gloved hand, he then performed an action-packed routine of twirling, twisting, and touchéing—with earsplitting yells to match. He even moistened the ends of the plungers and stuck them together and did a kind of plunger nunchuck routine. The whole thing was just a takeoff on the moves of the real karate experts. It was a lot of fun and the crowd loved it.

Buffer Golf

Everyone's out on the golf course while you play janitor? Not any more! It doesn't take much work or money to make your own genuine buffer golf course. Using a 14" or 16" 175 RPM buffer with a polishing brush or white pad, you can construct a "golf" skills course doing all the golfing with your buffer instead of a putter. We've used ours over and over again. Here's an illustration of how we made it.

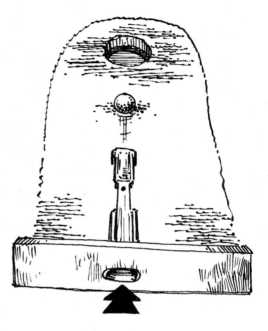

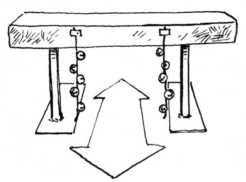

First hole, have the buffer "parked" inside a driveway between two ropes with bells hanging so that they give the "driver" just a small amount of clearance on each side. Golfers have to start the buffer and back it out without ringing the bell.

Here's another place where control counts. I mounted a drawer slide apparatus that goes through a "baseboard." A buffer on a fast swing hits the slide sticking out hard enough to knock the ball down the green into the hole—but it's no good if the buffer hits the baseboard. This gets three tries.

Cover a couple of 2x4's nailed together as shown, with artificial turf. Drill little 1/8-inch diameter holes along each board. Stud them with golf tees and balance a ball on each to make an alley the buffer driver has to maneuver through. Every ball knocked off is a stroke against you.

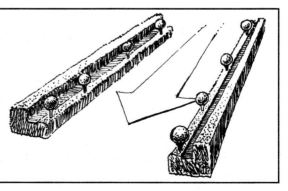

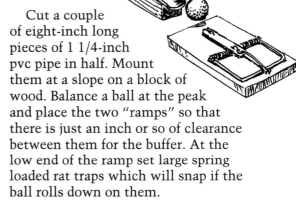

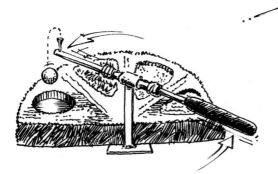

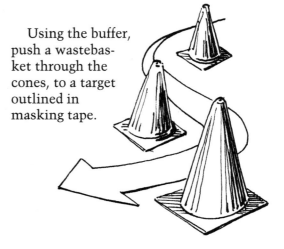

Cut a couple of eight-inch long pieces of 1 1/4-inch pvc pipe in half. Mount them at a slope on a block of wood. Balance a ball at the peak and place the two "ramps" so that there is just an inch or so of clearance between them for the buffer. At the low end of the ramp set large spring loaded rat traps which will snap if the ball rolls down on them.

The traps! Take a semicircle of plywood and divide it into four wedges with a hazard in each—water (a mirror), sand, rough, etc. Mount an arm that swivels in the center of the semicircle as shown, with a golf tee attached to the end. Contestants must push the arm gently with the buffer so that the ball clears all the hurdles.

Using the buffer, push a wastebasket through the cones, to a target outlined in masking tape.

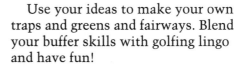

Use your ideas to make your own traps and greens and fairways. Blend your buffer skills with golfing lingo and have fun!

in Providence, pure Ivy League TP power, reached a towering 117 inches—the all-time record. Two TV cameras captured the event, and a big write-up in the paper let the public know that janitors have fun and are human and that the college trains and teaches professionals. Several college and company custodial meetings after that tied the record but the Wyoming Custodial Association, unwilling to allow those Eastern dudes to take their glory, rebounded with a dizzying height of 122 inches. That record stood until 1992 when (practicing all these years) Brown University, before my very eyes, made it 127 inches. (They had to turn off all the air conditioners and block off all breezes to do it.) One more way to show all those others out there that we cleaners are together, happy, and always training and topping each other to clean faster and better.

Stacking Toilet Paper

Ridiculous? Not by a long shot! Let me give you an example of how excellent use can be made of one of we custodians' most basic supplies—toilet paper. At one event, just to keep one section of a group busy, I tossed out a standard case of 96 rolls of tissue and asked them to see how high they could stack it. Soon there was a crowd doing it and others watching. It was a challenge—even the managers of the operation loved it! So I started including the stacking as a regular part of the fun section of our meetings or rodeos all over the U.S. Then a record 107 inches high was established by the Wyoming Custodian Association. The next year the record stackers got to 112 inches at the Hillyard convention in Minnesota. Then Brown University

Ten Creative Things to do with a Buffer Brush!

1. Make a clock
2. Have a snowshoe race
3. Make it into a mini skirt
4. Mount things on it
5. Use it as a roulette wheel
6. Make a planter base out of it
7. ... help me out here!
8.
9.
10.

Prize Stock Show

Here's another crowd pleaser: When fair time comes around, set up an arena with animals made out of cleaning equipment. It won't take much time or money to decorate different cleaning gear into a variety of prize livestock. (This is a great way to use up old, defunct, outdated, or damaged equipment, too.) Make up blue ribbons, and be sure the entries have nice big labels, too. Adults as well as kids will enjoy this display and it's a great chance to draw attention to the equipment used in cleaning. Few people appreciate the skill needed to operate cleaning equipment, and fewer still know what the machines are used for or for that matter that it takes some pretty complicated apparatus to clean up. Here are a few ideas—your employees could each enter an animal:

- scrubber buffalo
- buffer giraffe
- canister vac pig
- upright vac cow
- spray bottle turkey
- vacuum hose snake

…all made up of a variety of cleaning parts.

Vac Animal Contest

Have the cleaning people, using anything

to do with an old vacuum (any vacuum) create and bring an animal to the meeting. This went over so well in our company annual meeting that The Eureka Company held a national contest at the Riviera hotel in Las Vegas. Here's a copy of the entry form. Entries ranged from the very simple, like a snake made from vacuum hose, to the more complicated vac elephant. Some mighty interesting animals were made including: beetle, tarantula, gator, dog, armadillo, spider, gorilla, flamingo, and dinosaur.

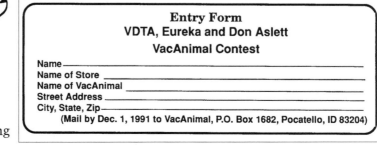

Rules and Entry Form For Don Aslett's VDTA and Eureka VacAnimal Contest

Who's Eligible: Entrant must be employee, owner or member of the family of a person who owns or is employed by an independent vac shop and who will be attending the January, 1992 VDTA Convention in Las Vegas.

Rules: Use any old vacuum parts, or parts from many vacuums (cords, insides, shells, etc.). Create a VacAnimal, real or imaginable, for the Vac Circus. Limit size to three feet by three feet and entry must be moveable, handleable, and manageable by one person. It cannot contain any electrical parts. The entry may be a reptile, bird, insect, mammal or an imaginary animal like a dragon or unicorn. Paint and decorate to your heart's content. No logos or manufacturer identification should be visible. You are responsible for set-up, assembly and shipping to and from the show. Your Animal is to be brought to the January VDTA Show and turned in, assembled at registration.

Name: Give your VacAnimal a name. Include a placard with the name for display, but don't put your identity on it. We'll assign it a number at the show. Here, for example, is *Piggus Compacti.*

Voting: Judging will be by ballots given to registrants at the January, 1992 VDTA show. Clever use of parts, color, humor, originality in names and design will all be considered by your fellow registrants when voting. Judging will be at the VDTA Convention Jan. 18-21, 1992, in Las Vegas. Awards will be announced at the keynote address.

And best: You get to keep your VacAnimal. After the show, you can take it home for display in your shop, media photographs, fun and sales.

Prizes: Prizes will be announced in future editions of VDTA News.

Entry Form
VDTA, Eureka and Don Aslett
VacAnimal Contest

Name
Name of Store
Name of VacAnimal
Street Address
City, State, Zip
(Mail by Dec. 1, 1991 to VacAnimal, P.O. Box 1682, Pocatello, ID 83204)

Janitor Jewelry

Can you imagine adorning yourself with motor parts and attachments and pieces from vacuums and other cleaning machines? Some stunning and unforgettable jewelry can be made out of cleaning items. If you don't believe me, come to my Cleaning Museum and see our display!

Cleaning Mailboxes

You'll be absolutely amazed what brilliant, creative, and humorous mailboxes can be made using pieces of cleaning equipment. Dispensers, mop buckets, vacuums, buffers—about anything can be painted and mounted and converted into a mail receptacle city or rural. Cleaning mailboxes are useful, fun, and speak out that we are proud of our profession and love what we do! Check with your local post office for the rules about positioning mailboxes.

Mop Art Contest

Every employee of my company was asked to make something out of mops. Soon we had mop dolls, birds, animals, people, all kinds of art objects— it's wonderful to see the creativity. Display these in a row and have a vote for the most original, prettiest, etc. Your people will never forget this. Many of ours are on display in

the world famous Aslett Cleaning Museum, including the famous Mop Your Heart bra, Willie Nelson immortalized in mopstrings, Cecil the Mop Sea Serpent, Princess Layflat, and Luke Skymopper.

Cleaning Furniture/ Lamp Contest

Our 1993 meeting in Homestead, Utah saw a vacuum hose recliner, Brute beach chairs, a baby rocker made out of buffer brushes, even a throne made from cleaning paraphernalia. I'm saving the lamp contest for the future along with a cleaning clock contest. (I'd love some new ideas, so please write me.)

Design a Stamp

At one meeting we held a contest to create a "Cleaning Stamp." The winner was a design of Elvis cleaning a toilet. (Just kidding.) Here is one entry.

Contest

Here is your chance to create a classy cleaning stamp! Here's the blank one for a rough and one for the finished product. Anything relating to "Clean" up our country-self, etc.

Varsity Contractors, Inc.
A Partnership for our future.
Building a Clean America

Create your own cleaning stamp! Make it as fancy as you wish!

PRIZE: $75.00 (Christmas money)

What Are Others Doing?

Custodial Olympics at the University of Kansas, Lawrence, Kansas—featuring 48 custodians dressed in t-shirts that said "Take the plunge."

Games from the World Series of Housekeeping, Opryland Hotel, Nashville, Tennessee.

Still other pro cleaners have come up with games and events like: Name that Tool, Measure Minders, Bed-O-Rama, Window Wipeoff, Dirtbuster Mania, Electrical Encounter, Plumbing Puzzle, Mop Magic, Buffer Driving Course, Stash the Trash, Soaked Sponge Relay, Tissue Torch Run, and Dust Mop Skiing.

I'd love to see what you are doing—please send me a note!

11 Varsity
Candid Shots

Annual Meetings:
A Chance to Upgrade &
Motivate in a Big Way

The last week of September is the
Varsity Annual Meeting where area,
district, and regional managers from
fifty states converge to learn the latest
in total facility services wisdom and
build team and individual strength.

The meeting consists of training
seminars, social time, fun antics and
special events, plus a community
service project.

2005: Tie Into Our Talent

Boise Idaho's Grove Hotel hosted the 2005 meeting that featured a resource tradeshow with over 30 booths representing segments of the company like the

Mall Division Construction, the Hospital Division, Marketing, Nuvek, and the Cleaning Center. Rotating from booth to booth participants learned about the many resources in our company.

A "Talent Show" was held and everyone wore their entries in the necktie and scarf competition made from facility services related items. The Tie Into Our Talent theme brought it all together.

2003: Varsity–Peace of Mind, Repeatable Success

In Park City, Utah the strategic theme was introduced: Varsity—Peace of Mind, Repeatable Success was the focus throughout the 2003 meeting.

The big event was the Pinewood Derby with over 200 cars entered.

2001: The Importance of One, The Power of Many

Pocatello, Idaho, home of the corporate office, hosted the meeting in 2001.

Varsity employees demonstrated the theme, The Importance of One, The Power of Many, by entering a brick representing themselves (right). Another contest was to make a Hawaiian Lei out of industry-related items (far right).

The Varsity Value Trail took attendees up the chairlift at Pebble Creek ski area. On the hike down they collected a bead from each station with a display representing these company values: Individual, Family, Country, Productive work, Character, Industry Image, opportunity, Success, and Excellence.

2000: Success–It's in the Bag

The golf bag that is! St. George Utah was a perfect choice for the 2000 golf themed meeting.

Pictured at right, are entries of a golf club, driver or putter, made entirely from total facility services items.

A team contest was to create a Putt-Putt Course in the shape of the letters TFS (below).

Twelve separate service projects like the one above, benefited shelters, the Children's Justice Center, and many individuals.

1999: TFS–Totally Fit to Serve

West Yellowstone Montana was the spot chosen for the meeting that focussed on being physically fit. The contest was to make exercise equipment from cleaning tools and supplies (below).

The service project was to clean the Union Pacific Dining Room (above), 6,600 square feet including huge log beams and natural stone columns.

Hans and Franz, Arlo Luke and Dave Hermansen make an appearance above.

1998: Catch the Vision of the Mission

In 1998 Varsity welcomed the Mall Division to their first company meeting. Held in Pocatello, the meeting focused on the mission statement. It featured a janitor rodeo, a garage sale to benefit the Portneuf Greenway, and perhaps the most fun contest ever, the Vacuum Cleaner Drag Race.

Above a scene from the garage sale. A buffer brush race takes off at right. Below the group photo along the Portneuf Greenway in Pocatello.

1997: 40 Years of Sharing, Caring and Learning

The Grand Opening of Varsity Square in Pocatello, set the tone with ribbon cutting and tours for the public and invited guests in 1997. The theme was 40 Years of Sharing, Caring and Learning.

Each district was assigned to build a training simulator. Above is a floor buffer simulator.

Sierra Pacific region provided musical entertainment.

1996: Total Facility Services

Total Facility Services was the theme for the 1996 meeting held in Jackson Hole, Wyoming.

Contests included Super Sombreros and the Great Janitor Soap Box Derby (aka Le Tour de Toilet). As you can see at right, not everybody made it to the finish line.

Varsity vendors are also invited to participate in the contests. Far right Dale Almond from Idaho Planning models his hat entry.

The Teton Science School was the beneficiary of the clean up project. The school gives over 5,000 students a year a hands-on approach to natural science, specifically the Greater Yellowstone ecosystem. Varsity refinished the lodge, screened and sealed the hardwood floors, and a list of other maintenance odd jobs.

1995: ISU Mini Dome

On Time for Quality was the theme for the 1995 meeting in Pocatello, Idaho.

Idaho State University's covered stadium has 12,000 seats—12,000 dirty seats! The Varsity team tackled the task of cleaning all of them in just 2 hours.

Beat the clock carried over into another competition: make a clock out of cleaning items (below)!

Part of the entertainment included sumo wrestling! At left is the t-shirt design for the Mini Dome project.

1994: Indian Rocks Scout Camp

The community service project for 1994 took place in McCammon, Idaho. The Varsity crew built a fence for the new scout camp here in a matter of hours. The theme for the meeting was: "Do It Right the First Time." Contests included Varsopoly, Cleaning Musical Instruments, and Cleverest Name Tags.

A life-size Varsopoly Game (see p. 130) included jail, OSHA infractions, bids, bidwalks, profit, loss, etc. At left is the theme t-shirt design for the 1994 meeting.

1993: Historical Catholic Church

Park City, Utah. The beautiful St. Mary's Catholic Church is on the historic register. For their 1993 community service project Varsity painted the inside of the sanctuary. The theme of the 1993 meeting was: "Call on Us—We're Ready."

Contests included making a flag representing your district, creating a janitor chair, "Manager Minute" talks, and a Policy and Procedures Exam. Plus a yearbook featuring a "personality profile" of attendees and spouses— background, hobbies, and family info on each to help employees get to know one another better. Below is the t-shirt design for the 1993 meeting.

1992: Historical Steam Engine "Heber Creeper"

Midway, Utah. The retired engine was cleaned and restored by Varsity in only 17 minutes. Theme: (appropriately) "TRAINING Program '92."

Below is the t-shirt design for the 1992 meeting. The cleaners also wore bandanas and engineer caps.

Employees entered a contest to build creations out of mops. Some entries are pictured here. And one evening Varsity hosted a Luau.

1991: Whiskey Springs National Forest

Heber, Utah. Varsity's project this year was to do repair work and painting, as well as build a barbecue and move signs for the Forest Service at this public recreation and camping area. The 1991 meeting featured a fine art contest, mop creations, and building the Varsity outhouse. How many janitors can you cram into an outhouse?

1990: Varsity Paints a Barn

Pocatello, Idaho. Varsity donned painter's whites and went to town, or rather the country, to paint the landmark Spanbauer Barn. The whole job was done in two hours flat (or semigloss).

Below, Arlo Luke, company president, arrives via limo for Varsity Night at the Movies.

Each district entered a 5-minute video production depicting life on the front lines of cleaning. This contest was complete with academy award presentations. At left, Don and Barbara Aslett arrive at the opening night gala.

1989: Clean a House in 10 Minutes!

Pocatello, Idaho. We did it, too—top to bottom in ten minutes! It was crowded, it was crazy, it was fun! The owner of the home, a victim of MS, was overjoyed.

The employee contest was to make an animal out of vacuums. Here is the Tyrannosaurusvac.

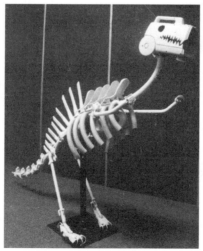

Each Varsity district made a section for a totem pole to be displayed at the home office.

Varsity Feud

For the Varsity version of the TV game show "Family Feud," the corporate office sent a survey out to employees and used the actual results in the game. Hilarious and surprising answers to basic operational questions showed managers where reinforcement was needed in the ranks.

Here are two examples:

How do you find out how to operate equipment?

Survey said:

Ask the boss/supervisor	18
Operator's manual	6
MSDS Sheets	2
Instruction on equipment	2
Ask manufacturer/sales rep	1
Try to figure it out myself	1
In my Varsity Handbook	1

What was your excuse for not coming to work?

Survey said:

I'm sick/family member ill	7
Overslept	7
Car broke down	5
Doctor appointment	3
No way to get to work	2
No one picked me up	2
Wife took car	1
Gone fishing	1
Mom died	1
Dog had puppies	1
Fight with girlfriend	1
Don't want to drive new pickup in the wind	1
Baby sick	1
Fear of vacuums	1
Dog died	1
Don't have a clean shirt	1
Been in a vehicle accident	1
No babysitter	1

Varsopoly

The life-size board game created to provide fun and inspiration, and at the same time teach our managerial team the ins and outs of our complex industry. There were board spaces that featured bidding, accident and loss prevention, managing contracts, employment issues, regulations, and benefits. The game included a mock courtroom and judge for WC claims and lawsuits, and much more.

The winner was the team with the most profit and contracts at the end of the game.

The board was made from twenty 4x8-foot sheets of plywood, colorfully painted as game spaces. We divided players into teams, each team having colored arm bands that matched their playing piece. Competitors were issued special Varsity socks to keep

from scratching the board as they moved around. Each team was given a starting packet of Varsopoly money, contracts, and rules.

A narrator/facilitator with a microphone rolled the dice, and kept the game moving.

When a team's playing piece landed on a chance or opportunity space, for example, they had to send a team member to the center of the floor to draw a card. The space marked "Advance to Bid Walk" provided an opportunity to obtain a new contract. The space marked Customer Complaint might result in lost money, or worse, the loss of a contract. The "Accident" space meant a lost turn, and the entire team sent to the hospital, with one member being put in a wheelchair, another on crutches, or bandaged up, etc.

Don Aslett's World Famous "Cleaning Museum"

How we used to clean and what we used to clean with is pretty astounding. Seeing it, touching it, or trying it out today can really focus one on how much better we cleaners—at home or in the business—have it now.

Collecting, labeling, and displaying some of that "old stuff"—equipment, tools, reading material, pictures, chemicals, signs, even urinals, can add spice to your department and profession. No one can resist "old" or "unique" and this will really get their attention. It helps keep people aware of what a major part of human life and history cleaning is.

Don started a full-scale museum for all of us in 1982, and it's grown to over 600 pieces now. It fills six rooms, and is located at Varsity Square inside the Cleaning Center, 311 South Fifth Avenue, Pocatello, Idaho. People are thrilled by it, and you are welcome to come visit!

We are looking for more pieces, so if you don't have a place or room for your own collection, become part of ours by donating your unique item to:

> Don Aslett's
> Cleaning Museum
> PO Box 700
> Pocatello ID 83204

Some items to be on the lookout for:
- Old hand pump (non-electric) vacuums
- Old buffers/scrubbers
- Old hand tools
- Unique, worn anything
- Old cleaning product containers
- Cleaning ideas that didn't work
- Mops/hand scrubbers
- Pictures, calendars, old cleaning ads
- Cleaning novelties and commemorative items, and souvenirs.

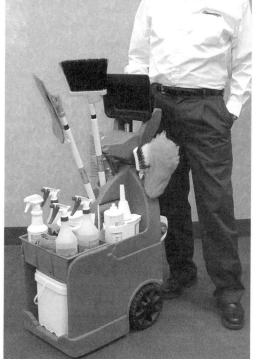

"Welcome to my world— the world of the professional cleaner!"

Come tour my maintenance-free house in Hawaii, and see my Cleaning Museum online at

www.aslett.com

Be a Professional Cleaner...

Cleaning up is big business, a 73+ billion dollar industry. It offers good income and a secure future.

Cleaning is also one of the easiest fields to enter. It requires very little start-up capital, yields an amazing 30% average return on investment, and offers the kind of life that will satisfy the dreams and needs of many who have been thinking of starting a business of their own: freedom of choice, attractive income potential, no special educational requirements, tax advantages, opportunities everywhere, and the chance to branch out into numerous related careers.

As a college student Don Aslett started cleaning houses to earn his way through school. That fledgling cleaning company is now a 250 million dollar enterprise serving all 50 states. Don gives seminars all over the country, and appears frequently on TV and radio. His many best-selling books include NO TIME TO CLEAN and CLUTTER'S LAST STAND.

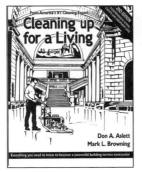

CLEANING UP FOR A LIVING

Is a complete, comprehensive, step-by-step guide to everything you'll ever need to know about the business. It's written in a down-to-earth, lively style that makes even the most "technical" subject easy to grasp and understand. If you want to investigate one of the many exciting specialties in the profession or explore the whole constellation of cleaning industry opportunities, *Cleaning Up for a Living* is the book you want. It will ensure that whatever branch of the business you choose turns out a success.

Includes 34 pages of forms of all kinds you can just copy and use.

208 pages, illustrated; $16.99.

HOW TO UPGRADE & MOTIVATE YOUR CLEANING CREWS

As someone who built a 250+ million dollar cleaning company from scratch on the strength of the enthusiasm and excellence of its employees, Don Aslett is in an excellent position to help you implement a motivation campaign for your crews.

In this book he shares hundreds of ways to uplift the image of "the cleaner" and motivate crews to take pride in their work. Get the benefit of more than fifty years of firsthand, frontline experience of what really works, and what doesn't when it comes to encouraging custodians.

144 pages; illustrated; $19.95.

THE PRO-FESSIONAL CLEANER'S PERSONAL HANDBOOK

The most comprehensive training manual ever for the frontline cleaner. You will learn here, from a master, not merely how to clean, but all the hidden and equally important "people" skills.

The first half of the book provides all of the important background information every cleaner needs. It begins by putting the cleaning profession into perspective, explaining the position of pride and responsibility it unquestionably is. The second half of the book is a complete guide to the actual "how-to" of cleaning, including how to organize yourself and your crew.

208 pages; illustrated; $19.95.

CONSTRUCTION CLEANUP

A guide to the exciting and profitable field of construction cleanup—cleaning and preparing facilities after the builders leave and before the tenants move in. How to do it efficiently and professionally, for new construction or remodeling projects.

• What to clean
• How to clean it

• Where to find jobs
• The equipment needed
• How to bid/price your jobs
• How to work safely
• How and why to keep the peace with others on site.

Plus all the forms and checklists you need!

116 pages; illustrated; $19.95.

"This book is well worth the money and I recommend it to anyone who is going into the 'construction cleaning' business."

DON ASLETT'S PROFESSIONAL CLEANER'S CLIP ART CD-ROM

CD-ROM with 240 black and white line drawings, from Don Aslett's own cartoonist. They'll bring life to your newsletters, flyers, cards, or brochures, anywhere you want or need a graphic depicting the greatest profession on earth.

240 illustrations on one CD; $29.95.

VIDEO: RESTROOM SANITATION

A complete video course in how to clean and care for restrooms professionally. Don's company, Varsity Contractors, Inc., uses this tape to train their crews to do a professional job. Produced by Varsity's Marketing Vice President, Jim Doles. Quiz booklet to certify your crews!

40 minute VHS tape, plus 40-page quiz booklet; $69.95.

PROFESSIONAL CLEANERS

CLIP ART CD

VIDEOS

TITLE	Retail	Qty	Amt
Clean in a Minute	$5.00		
Video Clean in a Minute	$12.95		
Cleaning Up for a Living	$16.99		
Clutter Free! Finally & Forever	$12.99		
Clutter's Last Stand	$9.95		
Construction Cleanup	$19.95		
Dejunk LIVE! Audio CD	$14.99		
Don Aslett's Stainbuster's Bible	$13.95		
Do I Dust Or Vacuum First?	$9.95		
Everything I Needed to Know About Business…Barn	$9.95		
For Packrats Only	$13.95		
Get Organized, Get Published	$18.99		
How to Be #1 With Your Boss	$9.99		
How to Handle 1,000 Things at Once	$12.99		
How to Have a 48-Hour Day	$12.99		
How to Upgrade & Motivate Your Cleaning Crew	$19.95		
How to Write & Sell Your First Book	$14.95		
Is There Life After Housework?	$11.99		
Video Is There Life After Housework?	$19.95		
Lose 200 Lbs. This Weekend	$12.99		
Make Your House Do the Housework	$14.99		
No Time To Clean!	$12.99		
Painting Without Fainting	$9.99		
Pet Clean-Up Made Easy	$12.99		
Professional Cleaner's Clip Art CD	$29.95		
Video Restroom Sanitation (includes Quiz Booklet)	$69.95		
Speak Up	$12.99		
The Cleaning Encyclopedia	$16.95		
The Office Clutter Cure	$10.99		
The Professional Cleaner's Handbook	$19.95		
Who Says It's A Woman's Job to Clean?	$5.95		
Wood Floor Care	$9.95		
While supplies last, FREE SAMPLE with purchase (one per household)			Free Sample

Shipping: $3 for first book or video plus 75¢ for each additional.	Subtotal	
	Idaho residents only add 5% Sales Tax	
	Shipping	
	TOTAL	

☐ Check enclosed ☐ Visa ☐ MasterCard ☐ Discover ☐ American Express

Card No. _____

Exp Date _____ Phone _____

Signature X _____

Ship to:
Your Name _____

Street Address _____

City ST Zip _____

MAIL your order to:
Don Aslett
PO Box 700
Pocatello ID 83204
OR Call: 888-748-3535
    208-232-3535
Fax: 208-235-5481

☐ Don, please put my name and the enclosed list of my friends on your mailing list for the *Clean Report* bulletin and catalog.

Upgrade 6/05

PROFESSIONAL CLEANERS

CLIP ART CD

VIDEOS

TITLE	Retail	Qty	Amt
Clean in a Minute	$5.00		
Video Clean in a Minute	$12.95		
Cleaning Up for a Living	$16.99		
Clutter Free! Finally & Forever	$12.99		
Clutter's Last Stand	$9.95		
Construction Cleanup	$19.95		
Dejunk LIVE! Audio CD	$14.99		
Don Aslett's Stainbuster's Bible	$13.95		
Do I Dust Or Vacuum First?	$9.95		
Everything I Needed to Know About Business…Barn	$9.95		
For Packrats Only	$13.95		
Get Organized, Get Published	$18.99		
How to Be #1 With Your Boss	$9.99		
How to Handle 1,000 Things at Once	$12.99		
How to Have a 48-Hour Day	$12.99		
How to Upgrade & Motivate Your Cleaning Crew	$19.95		
How to Write & Sell Your First Book	$14.95		
Is There Life After Housework?	$11.99		
Video Is There Life After Housework?	$19.95		
Lose 200 Lbs. This Weekend	$12.99		
Make Your House Do the Housework	$14.99		
No Time To Clean!	$12.99		
Painting Without Fainting	$9.99		
Pet Clean-Up Made Easy	$12.99		
Professional Cleaner's Clip Art CD	$29.95		
Video Restroom Sanitation (includes Quiz Booklet)	$69.95		
Speak Up	$12.99		
The Cleaning Encyclopedia	$16.95		
The Office Clutter Cure	$10.99		
The Professional Cleaner's Handbook	$19.95		
Who Says It's A Woman's Job to Clean?	$5.95		
Wood Floor Care	$9.95		
While supplies last, FREE SAMPLE with purchase (one per household)			Free Sample

Shipping: $3 for first book or video plus 75¢ for each additional.	Subtotal	
	Idaho residents only add 5% Sales Tax	
	Shipping	
	TOTAL	

☐ Check enclosed ☐ Visa ☐ MasterCard ☐ Discover ☐ American Express

Card No. _____

Exp Date _____ Phone _____

Signature X _____

Ship to:

Your Name _____

Street Address _____

City ST Zip _____

MAIL your order to:
Don Aslett
PO Box 700
Pocatello ID 83204
OR Call: 888-748-3535
208-232-3535
Fax: 208-235-5481

☐ Don, please put my name and the enclosed list of my friends on your mailing list for the *Clean Report* bulletin and catalog.

PROFESSIONAL CLEANERS

CLIP ART CD

VIDEOS

TITLE	Retail	Qty	Amt
Clean in a Minute	$5.00		
Video Clean in a Minute	$12.95		
Cleaning Up for a Living	$16.99		
Clutter Free! Finally & Forever	$12.99		
Clutter's Last Stand	$9.95		
Construction Cleanup	$19.95		
Dejunk LIVE! Audio CD	$14.99		
Don Aslett's Stainbuster's Bible	$13.95		
Do I Dust Or Vacuum First?	$9.95		
Everything I Needed to Know About Business…Barn	$9.95		
For Packrats Only	$13.95		
Get Organized, Get Published	$18.99		
How to Be #1 With Your Boss	$9.99		
How to Handle 1,000 Things at Once	$12.99		
How to Have a 48-Hour Day	$12.99		
How to Upgrade & Motivate Your Cleaning Crew	$19.95		
How to Write & Sell Your First Book	$14.95		
Is There Life After Housework?	$11.99		
Video Is There Life After Housework?	$19.95		
Lose 200 Lbs. This Weekend	$12.99		
Make Your House Do the Housework	$14.99		
No Time To Clean!	$12.99		
Painting Without Fainting	$9.99		
Pet Clean-Up Made Easy	$12.99		
Professional Cleaner's Clip Art CD	$29.95		
Video Restroom Sanitation (includes Quiz Booklet)	$69.95		
Speak Up	$12.99		
The Cleaning Encyclopedia	$16.95		
The Office Clutter Cure	$10.99		
The Professional Cleaner's Handbook	$19.95		
Who Says It's A Woman's Job to Clean?	$5.95		
Wood Floor Care	$9.95		
While supplies last, FREE SAMPLE with purchase (one per household)			Free Sample

Shipping: $3 for first book or video plus 75¢ for each additional.	Subtotal	
	Idaho residents only add 5% Sales Tax	
	Shipping	
	TOTAL	

☐ Check enclosed ☐ Visa ☐ MasterCard ☐ Discover ☐ American Express

Card No. _____

Exp Date _____ Phone _____

Signature X _____

Ship to:
Your Name _____

Street Address _____

City ST Zip _____

MAIL your order to:
Don Aslett
PO Box 700
Pocatello ID 83204
OR Call: 888-748-3535
         208-232-3535
Fax: 208-235-5481

☐ Don, please put my name and the enclosed list of my friends on your mailing list for the *Clean Report* bulletin and catalog.